Decatur High 1962 Class Reunion

Decatur Stories

The 1950s with Judy

Judy Reach LaRocca

JUDY REACH LAROCCA

TABLE OF CONTENTS

PROLOGUE

The move my Reach family made from Waycross to Decatur may have been one of the most memorable times of my life. The years from eight to sixteen surely were the ones that shaped my values, faith, appreciation of family, and my personality.

Now, the last trait may be the one that is most open to speculation and scrutiny. My personality was molded during those pre-adolescent and early teen years. Those also were the times my family began to change its dynamics and dimensions. Some moved away when they married or went to college, while some of us stayed right where we were.

Therefore, the 1950s became Judy's years and the ones that I am concentrating on in the tales and little stories throughout this book. These stories are all based on actual events in my life, not factual historical accounts. I will admit to doing something all Southerners are prone to do, and that is to add a little more salt to their bowl of Grits for better flavor. Facts and memories have merged into one teen brain full of stories.

The 1950s were years of political and social changes, yet it was also a time of high fashion and innovative architecture all of which stirred my soul. Imagination was bringing new inventions and creations that shaped the world.

This book is simply about a young girl's view of her life and family during the 1950s. Some stories are told in a conversational tone. Peppered throughout are pages about popular fashion, dance, music, even slang expressions and more in that era of change.

After finding my old diaries, scrapbook, and pictures a few years ago, this Decatur book fell right into place. Memories were awakened and my brain reacted. This book became a joy to write.

There should be lots of smiles, even some chuckles, perhaps a tear here or there, and even a few sympathetic nods. Many of these stories, hopefully, will help you remember your own teen years. After all, who we were and who we have become are based on our experiences, both good and not so good.

It was and is our own lives that matter in this world.

Dedicated to Patricia Ann Reach Cullens

My big sister gave love throughout her life sharing and building precious memories. She inspired me and gave me encouragement to write this book about Decatur as well as my first book about Waycross and our Reach Family. Her memories and love are cherished.

The Perfect Rose

She walks with grace, her spirit so high
Her charm, her wit, in great supply

Is this a flower I behold?
Perhaps it is a perfect rose

See her laugh, see her smile,
She shows her love all the while

This rose, each petal in gentle folds,
Does it hold a secret we should behold?

She smiles, she runs, her arms held wide.
She embraces us all with so much pride.

This rose so fragrant, so heaven sent
Is there more to find, just one more hint?

Her energy, her charm, her joy so free
She spreads her love for all to see

This rose, as it opens soon reveals
A beautiful heart and her soul so real

We know she is with us for her spirit glows
God gave us this gift, this precious,
Perfect rose.
by
Judy Reach LaRocca February 14, 2005
For my sister Patsy April 9, 1932 - April 18, 2005

ACKNOWLEDGEMENTS

My brother Kenneth Ashley Reach has helped me with memories and is a huge part of this book. Thank you for being my six-years-older-than-me big brother. These stories are told through my own eyes and surely will be different from your own memories, but they are Just Judy's Stories.

A special thanks goes to Sandra Wright and Joseph Stearman who gave me technical and creative support, especially for my www.JudysStory. com website

The following are a few of the friends and classmates who played a part in my life in Decatur in the 1950s. Some shared memories: others gave me story ideas, and all gave me inspiration for the book. Most are from the Spring Street and McKoy Park area, Fifth Avenue Elementary, College Heights, Fifth Avenue First Baptist Church, and Decatur High School:

George Mitchell, Bartley Snead, Neal Pharr, Shay Kneale, Linda Moss, Gail Carrington, Ann Bentley, Jean Haynie, Adele 'Posse' Cochran, Barbara Archer, Warren Neal, Pat Grogan, Jean Bellville, Billie Gae Selman, Janet Blalock, Janyce and Joyce McClung, Susan Huff, Betty Lide, Billy Rhodes, Bill Bridges, Larry Abbey, Ken Nation, John White, Carole and Ricky Kelly, Laura and Carol Elliot, Susan, and Harriet Kimbrell.

In memory: Blake McLeod, Jackie Hamilton, Judy Tatum, Martina Gifford, Johnny Lyons, Allen Callaway, Tommy Goddard, Dick Eickhoff, Joyce McClung, Darlene Goddard and all the other sad losses for the Decatur High Class of 1962.

CHAPTER ONE

Roots and Routines

"Judy, see if Daddy is coming down the street. I just saw Hortense flying over the trees heading this way!" My older brother Tommy yelled this to me as he hurried out of the kitchen letting the screen door slam behind him.

"William Thomas Reach, how many times have I told you not to let that door slam?' our mother scolded. She knew well that this would happen many more times, so she just shook her head from side to side.

"Sorry, Mama, I didn't mean to slam the door, and it won't ever happen again. I promise."

It was a half-hearted apology from Tommy, but at least he tried. He surely did not want her to be mad at him when Daddy was on his way home. Supper smelled good, and he wanted to eat it without somebody being mad or upset, which just made the food go down all wrong.

Avoiding that whole door-slamming episode, I ran down the sloping driveway to the street. Somehow, I had managed to keep my white shorts and pink blouse clean and halfway wrinkle free that day. *Wow, how did that happen?* Then I looked down at my sandals and saw that they were coated with thick Georgia Red Clay.

Rats, I thought as I scuffed my soles on the driveway to try to knock that glue-like dirt off the white sandals. Not bad, they now had that pinkish stain that we saw on everything in North Georgia. The sandy soil in Waycross had been easy to wash off, as I knew well. Most of the time I had been on top of, in, or had that South Georgia sandy soil all over me. Clay was different, it stuck.

Just as Tommy had predicted, there was our large Mallard duck Hortense. She was just settling her black and green feathers after alighting on her roosting place, the large granite rock in our front yard. After awkwardly balancing herself upon the angular gray rock, she had begun to preen her feathers with her large orange beak.

She knew she was pretty and wanted all of us to pay attention to her satiny-smooth feathers. Now she was ready to greet her friend. She loved our Daddy and made a satisfied grumble, while waited for him to give her the deserved thank-you pat for guiding him home.

Gazing up the street, I saw Daddy rounding the corner of McKoy Street. He was heading down Spring Street to the very end where our brick ranch house sat at number sixteen.

Daddy was making his way home from the trolley stop at Hill Street. This was the final lap of his daily routine after spending a long workday at The Capitol Building of downtown Atlanta. Catching sight of me, he broke into a warm grin, making his handsome face glow.

With the weather being so warm and muggy, Daddy had already taken off the jacket of his lightweight tan suit. He had it thrown casually over one shoulder and was carrying his black leather briefcase in the other hand. His hat was tilted back jauntily on his head giving him a dapper appearance, even after a full day of work. As he neared, I saw he had loosened his tie so I knew for sure he must be relaxed today. A calm supper awaited.

Hortense waggled her tail feathers and started making her hissing version of a happy greeting. Now my brother Tommy joined us, and we both gave Daddy a greeting. The three of us went into the carport to the side door of our home.

Looking back, we saw Hortense turning her head this way and that. Her afternoon chore had been completed, now she was beginning her other task as our diligent lookout. Good Duck.

Our brother Kenny was already sitting at the table. He was now a big teenager and did not feel the need to join us youngsters in doing everything. That was just fine, I still had Tommy for one more year before he entered the great vacuum of that *teen kingdom*.

Wait a minute, that shrewd Kenny was eating one of Mama's delicious biscuits, hot right out of the oven. That is why he stayed in the kitchen. Then I caught Kenny's sly smile with the meaning that he was now older and wiser than either of us.

I took daddy's hat, jacket, and briefcase, then he gave Mama a hug and a kiss. He always did just that and it always made me smile to see her smile. Their love for one another was apparent whenever they were together .

Sometimes, if it had been an especially busy or stress-filled day, she would visibly relax when Daddy embraced her. Then we all felt better, it was wonderful.

Supper was just about ready as the family gathered around the table. Now we could enjoy the scrumptious homemade meat leaf, mashed potatoes, and gravy that our mother had just prepared. I think I smelled crispy fried okra and of course her fluffy home-made biscuits, oh yes.

The Reach Family had once again taken part in our daily routine, showing how we had established roots in this town and this home.

We had a new life, new roots, and new routines.

CHAPTER TWO

Packing Up and Pups

The move from Waycross to Decatur was such a huge change for the Reach family, that some of us were filled with a little fear and some anticipation. It seemed the five members of my family that would be traveling in the car had totally different thoughts running through our heads. I just worried about my own head though, and boy, it was full of exciting thoughts.

The one very sad fact of this move was that my older sister could not move with us at that time. Patsy had a job with the South Georgia Infantile Paralysis Agency that had to be completed. Yes, it did take me a long time to learn how to pronounce and spell that, but I learned she worked for a good cause. I saw why she had to finish her work in Waycross. Guess a lot of people needed my sister because she was great.

Even though I knew this and knew what had to happen, I did not like it. Her job in Atlanta at Rich's Department Store would not start for a few more months. That meant there would be no Patsy in the car and no Patsy to join us when we reached our new home. *Patience*, Mother kept saying for me to have patience. I had better look that word up in the Webster's Dictionary to make sure it means what she wants it to mean. To me it meant *Wait Forever*.

Our oldest brother Roy Jr., had already been in the service, married Marjorie Barrow and was now a graduate student at Georgia Tech. He was getting an Electrical Engineering Degree and was doing well with his studies. He and Margie had been blessed with their first child, Stevie on January 26, 1952, and lived in the married housing section of Tech. We were all thrilled that we were going to be near them. I was an eight-year-old-first-time Aunt and now Mother and Daddy were grandparents for the first time. The whole family was happy for them.

There were two little additional travelers going on our trip who would make our move more fun. We had two tiny pups that managed to relieve any tension with their puppy antics. They licked faces, romped with one another, jumped from lap to lap, and rolled on their backs to have their pink tummies tickled. No one could resist laughing at them, even Kenny smiled, and he was not in an agreeable mood

Those two doggies that would be the first pets at our new home were our adorable Cocker Spaniel pups, one black and one tan. The tan one Daddy had renamed from Wilberforce to Ike as a tribute to Dwight D. Eisenhower, the new President in that year of 1952. *I like Ike* was heard everywhere in America, so the name seemed to be politically appropriate for the times.

Willie retained his given name since we all liked his name. Daddy had named all eight of our puppies beginning with the letter *W*, like Wilberforce, Wilhelmina, Wilford, Wallingford, and so forth. He was the king of dog naming with his cleverness and humor. Our Cocker Spaniel Honey had puppies of all colors just eight weeks prior to this move.

Oh, and I was able to watch all of them being born. When Honey started making a bed out of towels in our bathroom, Mother let her continue and added more to make her comfortable. Mama just knew how do things like that. She said we could watch if we stayed back and kept quiet.

"Honey knows what she is doing so she will not need our help, but I will be here just in case she does need me," Mama explained to us in a soft reassuring voice. We were worried about our sweet dog.

Honey seemed a little upset to me, so I *was* worried. Her belly had been so big I thought she was going to bust open. My eyes must have been opened too wide because Mama gave me a reassuring hug. Kenny and Tommy made a sound like *humph*, they weren't worried about anything. They were so big and tough nothing ever bothered them.

Soon those little packs of puppies began coming out and none of us said anything. I put my hands over my mouth and watched as Honey did take care of her puppies, just like Mama had said. One, Two, Three and Four.

I looked at Kenny and Tommy and they didn't look so tough, in fact they each looked a little sick to me. They both gave a shrug and said they had seen enough and were going to play some baseball. Yeah, sure.

My goodness it was really something. Honey was a very caring mother. By the time it was all over she had eight puppies, some with spots, some black, some tan, and all curly eared and adorable. I wanted to play with each of them, but Mama said I needed to wait until Honey had fed them.

Those wriggly, hungry babies wore her out. We had to hand feed some of them. It seemed that I was the only one who had fun doing all that. We made a milk mush and put it on a cookie sheet then thirty-two little puppy paws tromped in it. What a mess. There was always one pup standing right smack in the middle.

After that hullabaloo and the family getting attached to the puppies, we were told what had to happen. Honey had to stay in Waycross with our neighbor. It hurt all of us to leave her, but she was very tired. We were pleased Mother let us keep the two pups, but we sadly had to sell all the others.

Mother had been more than willing to make the move because of Daddy's new job, but it was much more than the job. He had a heart attack a year or so before this move that was quite serious. That was when our family thought we were going to lose our Daddy. We went through a terrible and worrisome time during the weeks he was in the hospital, then there was his recuperation at home. We had never seen our mother so deeply upset.

Because of the seriousness of Daddy's health, it was decided he could no longer be an active Revenue Agent. His job in Waycross as a Revenue Agent, entailed locating illegal Moonshine operations, then chasing those Moonshiners after blowing up their Stills. It was especially difficult if the stills were in the dangerous Okefenokee Swamp. None of that was good for Daddy's heart. We all thought it was exciting until we learned this difficult and dangerous work was harming his health.

Daddy had been fortunate to have obtained an excellent position at the Georgia State Capitol Building in Atlanta as a Special Investigative Agent in the Alcohol, Tax and Revenue Division. Yes, another long job title for me to learn. When would that ever end? He would still carry a gun, have a siren on his car, and carry a badge.

Even though we all understood why the move was necessary, it did not mean that leaving behind our Waycross life would be easy. For my mother some of her joys involved her love of gardening and taking care of her home. She had put a lot of work into making this a loving home for our big Reach family. However, she did not go without a bit, perhaps more than a bit, of complaining. She told us it was her *prerogative* to complain since she was being agreeable about moving.

That must be a powerful word to hold so much meaning because Mama sure took advantage of complaining. I must look up that big word in the Webster's along with the list that seemed to be growing. That will be the first book I unpack when we get to Decatur. I had a feeling I would accumulate a few good words on this big move

Mother voiced her complaints out loud, "I am sure the house is going to be too small. I must leave Thelma and my neighbors not to mention our church. How will they run Sunday School without me? Who will play the piano?"

"Roy, are you sure this home is going to be right for us? I should have come up to Decatur with you to buy this place, after all I have absolutely no idea what to expect. Does it even have a yard big enough for me to have a garden and flowers? I just don't know, don't know at all"

Daddy had begun his description of our new home by telling us about the large yard with many different types of fruit trees, flowering trees and shade trees. Mother was happy about that. He told her the front yard had Hibiscus bushes in bloom and Azaleas also. Oh, and a Mimosa tree full of pink blossoms floating everywhere that she would really like. There were big Chinaberry trees and what he liked best were the Peach trees full of juicy peaches ready to eat.

Well, between the peaches, the Mimosa tree, and the Hibiscus bushes Mother had given him a half-hearted smile. Her gardening green thumb must have started to twitch, and her brain must have started thinking of the flowers she could plant in the soil less sandy in a cooler climate. Yes, she liked the idea of that big new yard full of bright new plants.

It was difficult for Mama to leave the big white home Daddy had built just for her. It sat proudly on a corner lot at 607 Clifton Grove and was Mama's dream home. After all, they had found the perfect lot and planned their own home. There was a large living room with a fireplace and a separate dining room. The kitchen was generous with a built-in banquette large enough to seat all seven of us. There was a big, screened porch off the kitchen that held the wringer washer and led to the back yard.

Off the long hallway was a big bathroom and three good sized bedrooms with the master bedroom having its own fireplace. My brothers and I had great fun playing games in that hallway, even watching little Mickey Mouse cartoons. The telephone sat in a little cubbyhole in the hall where mother had lots of conversations on our party line with her friend Thelma Davis.

Oh, and there was a wonderful side screened porch off the living room with a swing where we spent a lot of time listening to Mama's imaginative stories. It was hard to beat that but beat that we would somehow.

Daddy knew what he was up against, a lot of pressure. He also was confident he had made the right choice for the whole family. He knew we would all gradually settle into our new life, we just needed to try to turn the page to start fresh in this new adventure.

He was the bright guiding light for our whole family. I loved and trusted his decisions and had always loved going on trips and adventures with him.

The Reaches were embarking on this adventure together as a family. It would work well.

Kenny, Tommy, Mama, Tom Shea, and Judy with 8 pups.

CHAPTER THREE

Dimensions and Drama

There were several reasons the puppies were needed as a diversion on that road trip from Waycross to Decatur in the year of 1952. Before we all began getting into the car, there had been the hectic time of getting the furniture loaded into the moving van.

We were told by Mama to gather our personal items and make sure any treasured items we had to leave behind found good homes. Although that sounded simple enough; it was not. I didn't own any treasured items. Well, what I did have would fit into my little suitcase, after all how much can an eight-year-old have?

Since Kenny had been upset about having to leave Waycross High School and his friends, he had not wanted to participate in any part of the move. Well, Daddy made sure we all did, I suppose. I felt bad about Kenny because although Tommy and I had a lot of friends, Kenny's were in High School and evidently that was different.

Tommy was agreeable about packing because he and I were looking forward to the new adventure of going to a big city. We knew we would always have our Waycross friends, yet Kenny was my big brother and I wanted him to be happy. Maybe when Tommy and I ever got to be teenagers we would know how he felt. Tommy was twelve, I was eight and Kenny was fourteen-years old years already. Then he finally told us he had a girlfriend. Well, even I could understand that.

Our 1950 Ford was *packed tight as sardines in a can*, as Daddy might have said. This car was very special to us. It was outfitted with a siren and painted a special chartreuse color, a yellowish green. It certainly did not look like the usual Black Government car Daddy had in the past. It was fast, dependable, and worked well for his undercover work. We really like all that. Daddy's job was exciting to us.

Daddy placed our personal items in the trunk. Kenny, Tommy, and I each had a suitcase and our pillows rolled in a blanket. We noticed Daddy was carefully putting some big boxes in the trunk. What were those? The movers had packed everything already; everything was out of the house. I mean the house was echo empty. We had yelled in it, so we knew it echoed. Then it became clear.

"Roy, be careful with my China and glassware. I wasn't about to let those rough movers handle them, and I am not about to have them get broken in our own car, for Heaven's Sake!" She fussed.

We all looked at each other. That was the *Personal Stuff*. We didn't have any, Mother had a lot. We better not say a thing and be careful around those boxes. We better be very careful.

Then we saw our Daddy give our Mama a big hug. She laid her head on his shoulder and her own shoulders visibly eased. Just like that, we could see her sink into his arms. That is how they were together. No matter what happened they were there for each other. I had tears in my eyes and my nose sniffled. I could not help it.

Sometimes I did not understand my Mama, yet I always knew she loved my Daddy and he loved her. We all knew that, and I loved my parents and my Reach Family.

Back in the car with our roly-poly pups, we were at last leaving. This departure had suddenly gotten difficult for everyone in the entire car. I heard sniffles, shoes scuffing, throats clearing, handkerchiefs being shaken and wiping tears away. Oh, wait that was just me.

It was all too sad, and suddenly I did not want to go. I had Cindy, Virginia, Sue Ann, Mary Kate, Gary and all our friends. Then there was the school playground, the church, the Green Frog, the nearby pool, and Laura S. Walker Park, just everything. Leaving our big white home on Clifton Grove in Waycross was suddenly way too sad.

As I have mentioned, Mother did not want to give up her gardening as she had always enjoyed her yard and her home. Our back yard was filled with paths lined with flowers and big Hydrangeas, Azaleas and Forsythia bushes. There was a bunch of stuff that was pretty, but I don't know what it all was. I knew I liked our whole yard that Mama had worked so hard to make lovely.

However, Daddy had not yet told our mother the exact dimensions of our sleek new brick ranch house sitting on the corner lot of Spring and Adams Street. Every room of the three bedroom one-bath home was much smaller than the large white home Daddy had built for us on Clifton Grove in Waycross.

Daddy knew what he was up against, a lot of pressure. There had been questions like, "Roy, how big is this new house? And don't tell me it is a three bedroom one-bathroom house again. I want to know the size of the rooms to know if my furniture will fit before we go," she insisted. She could insist.

This was the dreaded question Daddy had been waiting for and he had known it would be coming soon. Mama was a smart woman and would want to know such details before just packing up and hauling everything up to Decatur. Oh no, she was smarter than that.

He swallowed hard and said, "Well, Libby, now let's talk about this before you get too excited." Uh-oh, he knew immediately those were the wrong words to start that conversation.

"You are not telling me something about this house you picked out for our family. Just what is wrong with it. I knew it. Go ahead. Tell me." She uttered this with a glare and clenched teeth.

Yes, Mama was wound up then. She had her hands on her hips and her lips were pursed. She saved that pose for the children. I never saw her give that to Daddy. I had to hear this.

"Well, I think the bedrooms will be fine, Libby. I have already measured everything, and it will be all right. We were going to get bunk beds for the boys anyway and not take those iron beds and that big heavy chest," Daddy dared not take a breath as he continued.

"The double bed will go in the other bedroom and the dresser. And our mahogany four-poster bed and dresser will fit well," he said in his beautiful mild voice. Mother did not always fall for his mellow voice the way we all did.

"Roy Wheeler Reach, you are not telling me something. What about our living room couches and chairs and the radio?" she questioned.

Oh no, she used his whole name. That always meant trouble especially if I ever heard, "Judith Catherine Reach, what have you done now?" Even if I had not done anything, or at least thought I had not done anything wrong, those were serious words. She was not calling to give me a cookie, nope, it would be bad.

"Well, I think they will all fit except for one sofa. We don't need two sofas anyway, you said so yourself. There are fewer of us now." He hoped he had made his point. He never could be quite sure if his words landed as correctly as he planned.

"Hmm well, what about my Dining Room set, Roy? My Dining Room set means everything to me. My good China, my silver, my crystal all the things from my mother. You know these are precious to me." She had softened her voice and almost had a catch in her throat as if she was about to cry.

Daddy went over to Mother and put his arms around her tenderly and hugged her, not saying anything. He knew how she felt, and he knew when not to say anything. This is the one subject he had not wanted to touch.

"Libby, these new Ranch homes are not built like the formal homes we are used to with the large dining rooms. The table and chairs will fit just fine and the China cabinet, uh, but not the buffet," he finally said.

"Well, that is just not acceptable," she said. But instead of being mad, she began to cry. She sat on the floor and cried. Mother was not going to leave her treasured dining room set behind. She needed all the pieces because it held all her treasured items

My Daddy was a genius sometimes. He also loved my mother more than anything. Seeing her cry was too much to bear. We all could see that. Then an idea popped into his mind, he found a solution!

"Libby, look all I need to do is cut the legs off the China cabinet. Then place that on top of the buffet to make a very wonderful large China cabinet. Also, then there will be room on each side for the extra chairs," he was very excited about his solution and wanted Mother to be happy with it also. He waited for her answer.

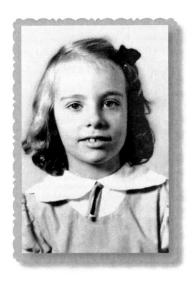

We could see the expression on her face when he said to cut off the beautifully carved and curved legs. She had inhaled with an audible gasp, putting her hand over her mouth. Her eyes were still wide as Daddy stood helplessly waiting for an answer. His last chance to please his wife in this important move decision.

She worked her mouth around. We could not tell if she was trying to keep from crying or what was happening with her face. Well, we never knew. We all waited with anticipation.

"Well, Roy, I guess that will just have to do, won't it? As long as I can have my China and silver and crystal all held safely and displayed, that will be fine," she said slowly.

Then Mother smiled. We all smiled. I think the entire world must have smiled. Daddy smiled the biggest!

It was on this very trip an incident happened that gave me a little more insight into my mother's colorful personality. Sometimes we were bewildered as her moods changed.

She was loving, funny, stern, opinionated, and smart. She was Mama.

CHAPTER FOUR

Mama, Me, and the Motel

Our furniture would not be delivered to our Decatur house until the next day which made it necessary for us to spend one night in a motel. We loved that, a motel, how much fun could there be in a motel? Mother seemed to be worrying more than being happy about the night ahead. Not sure what worried her, things had had been going smoothly the last few miles.

We found a nice place near Macon and happily piled out of the car. We had eagerly begun unfolding ourselves out of the backseat to check things out around the outside of the motel.

Look a pool, a play yard, vending machines, and our very own room to explore.

Daddy unloaded our luggage while mother was occupied with stuffing two puppies under her coat and scurrying into the room. Bam, the door was shut. She must have been in a hurry to get into the room.

"Mama, we want to explore outside, do we have to stay locked in here?" Kenny asked as if making a break from a chain gang.

"No, no, of course not, you three go check things out, but don't go far from the room. And please do not let the puppies out, do you hear me?" Mama must have been tired or something.

"Yes ma'am," we said in unison looking at each. We shrugged our shoulders and ran to explore our surroundings for the night.

We were so glad to be out of the car that anything outside sounded terrific. We found a Coca-Cola machine and managed to get two bottles with the coins Kenny had. Guess who had to wait for the leftovers. It did not matter because even a small sip of that bubbly cold drink was a treat.

We found the playground and pool. I was the only one interested in either, but the boys did humor me a bit. It was good to run around and not have either of them pushing and poking on me. We returned the bottles to the rack by the coke machine on the way to the room. We were in no hurry to go back to be cooped up in a small room. The car had been way too tight.

When we got back to the room, the beds had been prepared for us. Mama and Daddy in one, Kenny and Tommy in one, and I was on a cot, no surprise.

We were so worn out from the packing and the trip that we all fell asleep very quickly. Even the cot could not keep me from falling to sleep that night. I was used to cots from company coming to the house and having to give up my bed. If it was not a cot it was blankets on the floor, hard.

Suddenly something was shaking my foot. *What was that? What was in here? It was Mama.*

In a low whisper she said, "Judy, Honey, wake up I need your help."

Wow, she needed my help. I sleepily rolled out of the cot, which was very easy to do, and followed her into the bathroom.

She plopped down letting her white chenille robe with the pink puffy roses puddle on the tile floor. That action alone surprised me. Then I noticed the newspapers everywhere and the little blanket she brought from home. There were Ike and Willie in the tub with their paws on the rim, pink tongues hanging out and tails wagging. They wanted to play. It was three o'clock in the morning for Heaven's Sake.

Mother softly whispered, "When they saw me the two started whining and making a ruckus. I was afraid someone would hear them and tell the motel manager we had dogs in the room."

"We *do* have dogs in the room," I flatly stated. "Isn't that alright?"

"Well, now, Judy, you know how particular I am about following rules and doing the right thing. You have learned that well," she was smiling and giving me a compliment. What is happening in this motel bathroom in the middle of the night?

"Ike and Willie are not allowed in this motel, but it was the only one we could find. With all of us so tired we decided to take a chance and keep them quiet in the bathroom." She explained.

My eyes widened. "Mama, you are breaking the law. Are they going to arrest us? What will happen to the puppies? And why don't they like our Ike and Willie?"

"No, no Honey, it is not a law, it is just a rule this motel has for no pets. We will be gone in a few hours and if we can keep these rascals happy all will be fine." She said this in a very assuring voice. "It will be our little secret."

This was getting good. She was not only breaking a rule, but she wants to keep a secret with me. Me, the youngest and the one that nobody ever told anything. I always must sneak around and peek around to find out what is really going on around our house. This was great.

"Sure, Mama, it will be our little secret." Meanwhile we both had been keeping the rambunctious pups entertained and happy. They settled down at last and flopped over on their backs to fall asleep, pink bellies up.

I looked at my mother in a different way right then. Here she was with her hair all messed up and the bobby pins falling out around her. Her robe had gotten dirty and there were little rips where the doggies had nipped with their very sharp teeth.

Her face had a rosy glow I had never seen, like when she puts rouge on to go to church but this looked prettier. I liked her brown curls falling loose around her face. I looked at Mama and thought she looked prettier than I had ever seen her. In fact, she looked beautiful that night with two puppies sleeping with their bellies straight up and her smiling at them.

She looked as though nothing was wrong. There was not one crease in her face, and she had a soft smile. That was it! Nothing was worrying her at that moment. I wanted to fling my arms around her and give her a big hug, but something made me stop. Looking at her that night it did not seem right to spoil that moment.

Just then she reached over and hugged *me*, kissed my cheek, and said, "Thank you, Judy, you are getting to be such a big responsible girl."

She looked at me right in the eyes with a softness that made me feel nice and added, "You are very bright you know. I think you will like your new home and school and make a lot of new friends."

Wow, she had never said anything like that to me, ever. I just nodded because I did not want to say something dumb. I also had a lump in my throat.

That puppy time with Mother probably will be one of my best memories, or maybe not. I was only eight years old and had a lot to do and a lot to see, but it was wonderful.

There was Mama, smiling, happy, and taking care of Ike and Willie just as tenderly as she did when any of us were hurt or sick. I saw that tenderness when we watched her as Honey had delivered those puppies in our bathroom at home. Perhaps that is why she felt a special warmth towards the two pups. She had loved Honey dearly.

That night in the pink and green tiled bathroom there seemed to be a special bond, a bit of a secret held between us. She also had asked for and then depended on me for help. Maybe I felt a bit older and a little more responsible. Whatever it was, it was nice. I wanted to keep this night going just to have this one-on-one time with Mama, but I have a feeling this memory will last a very long time.

Ricky and Carole Kelly holding Willie and I have Ike

CHAPTER FIVE

Hortense the Lucky Duck

Our duck Hortense became more than our family pet, she became a neighborhood star. After all, how many people knew of a duck that hissed instead of quacked, chased dogs with the flap of her wings, wanted her beautiful feathers stroked, then strutted around like a guard keeping our yard safe.

There is an interesting story behind how we acquired such an unusual pet as our duck. You see, one day a flock of migrating ducks flew over McKoy Park, just beyond our back yard. Kenny, Tommy, and I had been watching them as we held our hands above our eyes to block the sun's glare. The flock had made a perfectly V-shaped formation.

Suddenly one duck seemed to break away from that perfection in their flight pattern. We watched as it began to falter and flutter, falling away from the flock. As the ducks came nearer to where we stood, the faltering duck dropped lower and lower. It was quite evident that one wing was hanging down limply as the duck tried in vain to stay aloft.

"Oh, no, that poor duck. Look, it's hurt and can't keep flying." My eyes were now tearing up because I could not stand to see any animal or creature hurt.

We knew it was in trouble, so my brothers and I quickly ran down the clay bank on the back of our yard. We crossed over to the baseball field where the poor duck was now struggling to land.

"Stay back you two. Don't make any noise." Kenny was taking charge of this rescue mission.

All of us kept our distance to not frighten the injured duck. We were close enough to the place where it had landed to see this was a beautifully colored Mallard. One of its wings, a shiny black, green, and white wing, was splayed awkwardly on the ground. We had to somehow help this creature.

"Should I go get something to make it easier to carry?" Tommy suggested.

We all tried to think how best to help this duck. "He's going to die, isn't he?" I was starting to hamper the mission with my questions.

Tommy and Kenny seemed to know what they were doing. "Judy, just stay back a little and let us see if we can help this duck. It's wing looks bad."

Tommy said this in what he wanted to be a calm voice, but the words came out an octave too high. He was upset. Even though we were trying to quietly approach the duck, we heard it begin to hiss, not honk or quack, and it was quite intimidating. Had this poor thing lost its quack-ability in the fall?

"What in the heck was that noise?" Kenny asked. "I never heard a duck hiss. Something is really wrong with this thing."

We bravely persevered and gradually gained the injured duck's confidence. At last Kenny was able to reach under its body so he could gently pick it up to take it home.

This duck did not understand gentle and kept pecking away at Kenny's arms as well as Tommy's hands when they tried to help. "Dang that hurts. What the heck is this thing doing?"

"Ouch, this doggone duck is pecking at my hands. Hold him tighter Kenny," Tommy pleaded.

"I'm holding it as tight as I can without squeezing the gosh darn thing. Keep your hands out of the way, Tommy. You are not helping. Just keep moving." Kenny's frustration level was reaching a breaking point. This was quickly getting out of hand for us.

Oh my, this was some duck, a pecking, hissing, flapping aggravating duck it seemed.

I stayed out of that mess. The duck was obviously mad about having a hurt wing and probably frustrated because it had also lost its quack. Not a good day for this duck. Nope not a good day for any of us.

Our ever-ready-for-anything Mother had already gathered a fix-it kit. She was standing at the edge of our back yard and had been watching the ordeal that was unfolding on the baseball field.

She always kept a vigilant watch over what was going on from her vantage point of the kitchen window. She could see our back yard, the Greenhouse, the Pool, the Park, some of the Skating Oval and the Whole Baseball Field. Of course, she saw what had happened!

We heard her say, "Well, at least it's not a mangy mutt this time."

Then our calm and practical mother first held the duck's beak tightly in one hand to keep it from pecking and hissing. How does she always know how to do this stuff and why didn't we learn this sooner?

Kenny and Tommy were relieved to have the pecking hissing duck in someone else's hands. Theirs hurt.

Mama showed us how to help bandage the bent wing. The duck had finally settled down to a mild wiggle. It was letting her tend to his hurt wing.

I'm thinking right then, "Just wait until Mama finds out this duck lost its quack or honk. What will she do about that predicament?"

At last, the poor creature began to overcome its initial fright and seemed to quiet down. Once again Mama calmed the situation. Or perhaps it knew these large two-legged creatures that had two skinny wings with no feathers were helping her. Those strange featherless wings had a firm grasp.

For whatever reason, this lovely duck became accustomed to us and began to waddle around more confidently. As its confidence grew so did its attachment to our family. Soon this lame duck became our companion. I gave up on ever hearing it quack and learned to like the various hissing sounds.

Daddy had named the large Mallard Horace, for with its brightly colored feathers it must be a drake. Then in the next day or two Horace laid two big eggs!

Daddy then renamed our duck, Hortense; and that was that. This magnificent duck was now our family pet with a perfect name. Also, *Horace's* eggs never did hatch.

We gave her a large tub filled with water that Daddy put into a hole. It was like a little pond. She loved the doghouse that she could sleep in, as needed. When her wing began to heal, she would flutter up and land on anything handy: a branch, a porch rail, a ladder, or any place where she could perch.

Now that we saw she was healing, we just knew any day she would fly away. When a migrating flock flew over the following year, we were prepared for her to take flight and join them. But our now family pet Hortense stayed.

She soon began to fly higher, then to soar as she watched below. That is just how she learned to sense when Daddy would be coming home. She would circle above the trolley stop and slowly fly above the street and above the trees. As Daddy wound his way home on foot, Hortense accompanied him in flight. It was truly an amazing sight to watch.

Daddy loved watching her and we loved our Happy, Lucky Duck

Tommy and Kenny work on Basketball set up as Hortense watches

CHAPTER SIX

School Days and Spelling Bees

My eagerness for going to school began in Waycross where we lived just across the street from Williams Heights Elementary. It would be easy to walk across the street to attend the first day of school if that day would ever arrive. Since age three or four, I had watched my brothers Kenny and Tommy going to school every day and coming home in the afternoon. They were four and six years older than I was and seemed to be able to do lots more neat stuff than little sisters did.

When I finally grew tall enough to climb the big oak tree in the corner of the yard, I would settle into the crook of a branch for the best vantage point to spot my brothers. Sometimes I would take a book or a peanut butter and jelly sandwich. The book could easily be stuffed into my overalls, but the sandwich usually got squished; no matter, I ate it anyway and waited.

Mama, my sister and brothers had read to me so often from many books and the Compton's Encyclopedia, that I already knew how to read before going to school. Mother had taught me how to spell, especially my middle name of Cat-Her-In-with an E, Catherine. The Compton's set was on a low shelf in the living room so I could pull one out anytime and enjoy.

The pictures with some of the stories were fun and even better when I could read the stories myself. I loved those books and all the glorious information found there.

Would my day to go to school ever arrive? Yes, it would and when that day finally arrived my mother barely had tied the final loop on the bow of my dress before I dashed out the door. Running across the road to that big red brick schoolhouse to finally being a student was really exciting.

"Judy Reach, slow down, you are too early," Mama cried out. Her words died in the dead air. I was already on the school grounds.

Standing on my tiptoes to pull on the big school door handle, I could not get it to budge. *This door is heavy!* I thought to myself, to my first-grade eager self. No, the door was not heavy it was locked, I was too early. The school bell had not yet rung so I sat down on the top step and waited. Soon both the doors did open wide behind me and were propped open.

With a big smile I stood and began saying hello to the kids starting to arrive, realizing I already knew just about everyone. They were my friends.

Hey, wait a minute, it looked as though I was a greeter or something, not a student. I quickly began following behind the others to enjoy the excitement of finding our classrooms and sitting down at our desks. Nobody was sitting, everyone was moving and talking because we did not know what to do. This was our first day of school ever. All this hullabaloo took place in about one minute.

The teacher had been at the door of the classroom during that long minute. She entered her classroom and we all hushed and scrambled to sit down at the desk we happened to be standing beside. Oh, what a sweet smile she had, a sweet silent smile. Was she ever going to talk to us?

"Students, I want to welcome you to your first day of school here at Williams Heights Elementary," the lady said in a voice not too loud. We all began to move and shuffle our feet around excitedly. She raised one hand.

"Now Class, there will be no more of that moving around in or out of your desk. First, my name is Miss Ledford, and this is how to spell my name," she spoke these words in a louder voice that we could tell meant she wanted us to pay attention.

Ending up on the second row in the middle of the classroom was just right because I could see everything. Wow, she could write on that big blackboard in a neat way and her letters were easy to read. I wanted to learn how to do that.

There I was smiling and looking around then noticed I was the only one smiling and looking around. What was that all about? Oh well, I turned back and put my chin on my hands and continued to be under this lady's spell. When I leave today, I was going to say *Hello* to her.

And so began my love of school and my love of being friendly to my classmates. It was easy in Waycross where my *schoolmates* were my *playmates*. Then after the second grade ended came the big move, the big change in my family's life. We left the South Georgia hometown of Waycross and moved to the North Georgia Atlanta area.

Almost immediately I loved everything about our new adventure. New house, new city, new school, new church, and new friends, I loved it all. Naturally the first day of school at Fifth Avenue Elementary was one that was more of excitement than worry, well maybe just a little worry. Everything seemed very different up here.

Mama and I met with Mrs. Bradford, the Principal to get acquainted with the school. It was a large red brick building with all the classrooms on one level plus a big auditorium with a stage, I liked that. On the bottom floor was the cafeteria that opened out to a huge play yard and ball field. Oh no, it was all covered in red clay and hilly,

Waycross was flat. Mother squeezed my hand. We were both thinking the same thing, too much red clay, too many stains on clothes.

She had already gone through this first day meeting with Tommy, so he was settled into the seventh-grade class just fine. I am sure he did not even notice the red clay, after all he was a boy.

The principal was a tall lady, well, taller than my mother. In fact, I decided that I would do whatever she said I should do, and quickly. Even her shoes clomping on the wooden floors demanded authority, not in a mean way because I liked her. When I looked up to see her, I looked way up. But I was only eight years old and lots of people looked tall to me. In fact, I stood back to see her better and smiled.

Mrs. Bradford told me my teacher would be Mrs. Donaldson in the third-grade class. After the tour she shook my mother's hand, telling her she would take me to my classroom. I looked back at Mama who gave me a smile and a wave. She also motioned that I needed to straighten the sleeves and ruffles on my blouse. She had sewn this pretty outfit for me, so she wanted me to look nice today. Smiling back, I adjusted the blue ruffles and straightened the sleeves, then smoothed the pleated skirt. Mama was gone, I was on my own.

Then it was only me and the tall lady clomping and tapping down the wooden hallway, the long hallway to somewhere. Oh yes, here we were as I rounded the corner into my new third-grade classroom. There was Mrs. Donaldson and all those classmates who I would be with for the next five years. *Hello*!

And oh, those kids, those friends, those pals, those oh so important people in my life. They became more than, Good Morning, Hello, and Hey, they would move up with me each grade until it came time for us to graduate from seventh grade then up to High School. Most of us would go to Decatur High School, others might move away, or go to another school.

In High School we would no longer know who would be in any of our classes. Many Decatur elementary schools were joined together in High School. There would be no guarantee any of us would be together again. Naturally, a lot of us wondered about our futures. We all were also excited at the prospects of our future days together.

The next week I slid into my desk, took the blue ink jar from the cubby hole beneath my desk and placed it in its little hole in the top right of my desktop. Then I put my sharpened #2 yellow pencil in its groove and finally opened my three-ring blue notebook to the arithmetic page. Arithmetic was fun and I was glad to start the day with my favorite subject.

The English, Geography and History books just filled the desk's cubby hole. Suddenly there was a little kick on my foot from behind me and looking back there was George giving me a big grin.

Oh, I felt my blush beginning again. Between the freckles and the blushing of my cheeks there was no hiding the fact that I thought George Mitchell was a neat guy. He was really cute, and he had a cowlick that suddenly popped up on the top of his thick head of hair. He tried to comb it down with his fingers but *poof*, the stray hair popped up again. It was very cute.

Sarah Kneale sat next to me and that pleased me. We had become good friends right away when we moved to Decatur from Waycross. I felt happy and secure to start my day right where my desk sat.

After Arithmetic we had English. We were learning how to diagram sentences into subjects, adjectives, verbs, adverbs, and predicates. I liked the way the sentences looked when drawn in the diagrams, but I was ready for that to be over because today there would be a Spelling Bee.

We had those in Waycross too. I liked them then and now. The class was divided in half with a line by the windows and a line on the opposite wall. Miss Donaldson slowly pronounced each word and used it in a sentence. *Cafeteria*, followed by a sentence, "We will soon go to the cafeteria to eat, cafeteria."

With each turn someone would spell or misspell their word and sit down if they missed. Some of the boys would scuff the toes of their shoes if they missed when it got down to ten students. I was very competitive about spelling and really liked to win. The final Bee usually came down to four of us. My stomach churned because the words were increasingly more difficult.

Oh no, how did this happen? It had gotten down to just between George and me. If I won, would he be mad at me? If I lost, would he act too proud?

"The person that spells the next word correctly will win."

"*Accidental*," Miss Donaldson spoke. "Is it accidental that Judy and George are the last students standing?"

The class laughed and it broke the tension for me as George and I both smiled. It was my turn first and I knew this word. "A-c-c-i-d-e-n-t-a-l, accidental," I confidently spelled.

"Correct, Judy, you have won the spelling bee today. George, maybe you will be first next time, second is very good. I am proud of all you students today. George smiled and shrugged his shoulders. All was good.

Then we all went to lunch, and after that we were a little tired, so Miss Donaldson let us read the books we had chosen. I loved to read books, so this was a treat to me. Looking around I noticed most of the kids had their elbows on the desk with their head on their fists, about to nod off. Oh well, too bad if they didn't want to read these exciting Nancy Drew Mysteries, or Tom Sawyer. It was their loss.

We ended the day with our Geography lesson and found that we were going to have to make a project for a school fair. We could use any country we wanted, but had to talk about their flag, crops, industry, and population. Also, we had to make the country true to its geological make up. That meant showing mountains, lakes, rivers, and cities.

Lots of groans traveled throughout the classroom. Miss Donaldson rapped the desk with her ruler and said, "Quiet down now. You have three weeks to finish this, and you can have time in the library to study your country."

Then in an unusual concession for such projects she added, "For this one project, you will be allowed to have your parents help with the paper and glue part to make Papier Mache. With that you will then need to make the mountains and landscapes."

"Yay," started going around the classroom, but she put a quick stop to that. "Now you must do all the design work and research yourself, remember. Your parents can just help with the messy work. Do you all understand?"

"Yes Ma'am," came our low unified reply.

When the final bell rang a miraculous feat occurred. All the students had their books in hand and their feet ready to step from their desks. Amazing how all those students could fit out one door, go down the hall in a fast walk, with no running, out the double doors and down the stairs in a matter of seconds. It took a lot longer that morning to get everyone who dribbled in and plopped down in their desks with little enthusiasm to start the day.

This was a how a normal day in the third grade at Fifth Avenue Elementary School went in 1953.

CHAPTER SEVEN

Big Brother, Curves, and Cursive

One morning I was waiting for the bell to ring at Fifth Avenue, knowing I could not be late for class. Daddy had taught us that punctuality was important in all situations to show you have respect and good values.

Just as I was about to enter the third grade classroom, two older girls started walking toward me, right toward me, and I wondered why. I was a new student but thought these two must be seventh graders. They were tall and pretty.

The blond girl had a big bouncy ponytail. She was wearing a straight skirt, a tight skirt that hugged her curves. Topping the skirt was a bright pink sweater that equally hugged the rest of her curves, and a pink scarf to finish her outfit. Would I ever look like that or was I destined to have this straight up and down no shape forever? My brain was getting off track of the present situation.

Her friend had beautiful dark hair done in a neat page boy curled under perfectly. I could hardly keep my eyes off her lips though, they were bright ruby red. What made her stand out even more was the ruby red dress she was wearing. Visions of Little Red Riding Hood kept popping into my head. *Concentrate, Judy, this could really be something important.*

Maybe they sent upper classmen to check up on us younger students. Was my skirt crooked? I looked down at the navy-blue full skirt perfectly ironed as Mama had done. I reached up to my pig tails and both blue bows were neatly tied. Was my white blouse unbuttoned? No, and my white socks were folded nicely, and my laces were tied. So, what did I do?

They both came to an abrupt halt right in front of me. Blondie's pony-tail began to bounce up and down as she asked me hurriedly, "Hey, are you the little sister of Tommy Reach?" She asked very excitedly, like it was a big deal.

Oh no, was Tommy hurt or something? I asked myself. "Well, yes, I am his sister." Will I always have the Little Sister Label?

"Neat-O! He is just so dreamy, and we wondered if he had a girlfriend yet, since school just started," she asked with hopefulness.

Dreamy, she thought Tommy my brother was dreamy? What did she want me to say? "Well, yeah, he has several girlfriends."

Wow did I just tell them someone died? Their faces froze in disappointment and their mouths gaped open. Now the Ruby Red Lips looked like a big red-letter O.

Oh, dear now I've done it, I have struck them speechless! I had heard of this happening before, but never imagined I could be the cause of such a strange reaction.

Trying to ease the situation I added, "He told me there were lots of girls in the seventh grade and lots of guys too who were becoming his friends. Tommy likes everybody," I boldly added.

You would have thought I had given them a box of chocolate candy because they both grinned and sighed at the same time.

"Oh, that's just super! Yes, he is very nice, and he does seem to make friends easily. Thanks, ah what was your name, Jodie?"

Jodie, do I look like a boy or something? I quickly told them firmly, "My name is Judy."

How could they think I was a Jodie, and what kind of name was that in the first place? No one in Waycross was named Jodie, and anyway I like my name, so I repeated, "Judy, I am Judy Reach."

"Sure, sure, thanks." Both girls giggled with their hands over their mouths and quickly rushed into the seventh-grade classroom.

That was weird, but at least I was not late for my third-grade class. Gradually the strange encounter with those girls faded and I was able to concentrate on class again. It was a good day and things were going well.

Suddenly it occurred to me what was next. We had to write longhand on the blackboard, and it would not go well for me. Why did I have so much trouble learning to write cursive? I liked to print and when we used the lined notebook paper it made the letters stay nice and neat, well, neater. My hand-writing looked better on that lined paper also.

Mrs. Donaldson asked for a volunteer to erase the board and then draw the four lines for us to use for writing the letters. Blakey raised his hand where he was sitting in the second row. Look at that Blake McCloud, I thought to myself, *there was another cute boy in this class*. He always had a little swagger when he walked, like he was cool. He was.

Oh, he just looked at me, yes, he did. I looked over at Sarah and we both smiled. She knew he was cool too. Well, several people were asked to write their first and last names on the board but the next time with no lines, just a plain blackboard. This will not be good for me. And the day had been going so nicely, now this.

"Judy, it's your turn to write your name on the board."

"Yes Ma'am," I said a little too quietly, but slowly slid out of my desk and walked to the big beast, the blackboard.

I picked up the chalk and started out with my nice big loopy *J*, then started the smaller *u* and connected the *d* and finished with the *y*. As I looked at what I had written there was a noticeable slant downward, and each letter got smaller somehow. Oh no, this is bad. I made a big loopy *R* then connected the *e* and the *a* and the *c* and finally the *h*. Both words looked like two broken seesaws, not a good thing.

Well, go ahead let me have it, I glumly thought.

"Now Judy, you are such a bright young girl in all your subjects, why does your cursive writing look like that?" Miss Donaldson asked.

"I don't know, Ma'am. I practice at home but do better on the lined paper." Saying this as if that was a good excuse for seeing my name headed off the bottom of the blackboard where it would land on the floor in a pile of messy letters.

Then she said it. She really said it. She said the words that I probably would never be able to forget, never ever forget.

"Judy, I hate to say it, but your handwriting is *stingy*, like you don't want to share it with everyone," she stated without a smile.

Oh no, I wanted to hang my head and could feel tears welling up in my eyes. *No, No, No! I am generous, not stingy. I am Judy, I do not cry in school.* So, I didn't.

Being a sensitive teacher, Miss Donaldson said, "All right children I think this is a good time for recess. Put your books away and file out to the playground quietly in the hallway. Remember to use your soft voices while inside the school."

Good Golly was I glad to hear those words! Perhaps my reputation as a good student would not be ruined. As I lined up with Sarah, Linda, Susan, Becky, Janyce, Joyce, Cynthia, Betty, Dorinda, Joy, and the rest of the class, I already was feeling better. The boys always seemed to trail behind the girls.

Someone got out the big jump rope and we started taking turns jumping with one or sometimes two at one time. I was feeling better. Recess was always fun because you could play and be loud if you wanted. Just running around in circles would have made me feel better right then.

Then I looked over at the opposite side of the field and spotted Perky Ponytail girl and her friend Red Riding Hood Red Lips. They had Tommy trapped while they twisted their hair and swayed their hips. He managed to escape and ran over to play football with the guys. He was good at sports and really liked to toss the football or start up a game of baseball.

Curvy girls again looked disappointed. I had a sneaking suspicion they were just beginning their ploy to get my big brother for a boyfriend.

Tommy was smiling and laughing. Then he happened to catch my eye and quickly turned back to the game. No eye contact allowed with sisters on the field. That was OK because Tommy and I always got along really well, and he would be there if I needed him.

I had to admit that I liked having Tommy as an older brother because he was a great guy and nice to everyone. I had learned and would continue to learn a lot from him. Next year he would be going downtown to Decatur High School. I liked knowing he was in school with me right then.

When a lot of us sat down on the hill to talk I told them about the two older girls talking to me that morning. They each thought that was surprising as they usually acted snobby and ignored all the younger kids.

Then we started talking about Tommy's teacher, Mrs. Selfridge. Everyone else knew her since they had been going to Fifth Avenue since first grade. I had seen her fleetingly as she was entering the classroom.

"Oh, you don't know about her? Well, we will have her in four years as our own teacher," Betty said. My brother Millard is in her class too.

"She has been teaching seventh grade for bunches of years." I could see the other kids giggling and wanted to know what was so funny.

"Well, she has a few little tics with her face," Susan added.

"Ticks! She has ticks on her face?" I blurted.

They all laughed, and someone said, "No, twitches, like she blinks and squints one eye. It's hard to keep your eyes off her face, so she probably thinks everyone is paying close attention to her lessons."

"It sounds as though she does more twitching than teaching," I commented.

"Yes, I know, but even with all that, her students say she is a good teacher, just quirky. In fact, her students come out of the seventh grade better prepared for the eighth grade than many other schools." The other girls nodded in agreement.

I am thinking the whole-time people are telling me these tales that I must ask Tommy a lot of questions when we get home. Tommy rode his bicycle to school with the older kids, so he left for school after I started my walk and then got home way before I did.

Since there was no intermingling between older brothers and little sisters at recess, I had to wait to see Tommy. That brother-sister rule must be written down somewhere. Should I tell him about my encounter with Pony-Tail Girl and Red Lipstick? I think not. He didn't look so happy when they had him corralled.

Oh, there was one more off limits place for any acknowledgment of siblings, and that was the cafeteria. That was a social gathering place for students, so there were important guidelines and pecking orders for seating and eating.

If some of us did not use the cafeteria, we would bring our lunches from home. I brought mine in a Doris Day lunch box with a red thermos. Mama made great sandwiches like pimento cheese, peanut butter and grape jelly, bologna and cheese, or pineapple and cream cheese. She wrapped all the food neatly in waxed paper and even included a cookie, apple, or banana.

Sometimes we were able to buy the little ice cream cups with the little wooden spoons for a treat. The kids who paid to eat the food served in the cafeteria did get a hot meal, but we liked Mama's lunches better. Tommy had to have a plain brown sack though, not a sissy lunch box like us girls.

That day I rushed home to talk to Tommy about what those girls had told me.

"What are they talking about, and why do you listen to them?" he quickly asked with irritation in his voice. "Mrs. Selfridge is a terrific teacher, she's tough, but makes us study and learn," he continued. Still with an edgy tone.

"But what about the ticks on her face, or twitches or something like that?" Just hearing myself say that made me feel foolish. I should have used my head better, but my head was only eight years old and wasn't filled with as much brain power as Tommy's twelve-year-old seasoned one.

"You will see when you get to seventh grade and have her for your own teacher. " His voice was softer now, like he really cared.

"Look, those girls, especially the older ones, love to spread rumors and exaggerate the truth to a new student."

He looked at me then and seemed less irritated, "I just want you to understand that, so you don't keep yourself upset," he finished in his usual nice voice.

I thought a second about all he said, before saying anything, which was an unusual action for me. Finally, I said, "Gosh, Tommy I feel silly now, but thanks for telling me all that."

Tommy was ready to get to High School. He had to endure flirty girls, avoid his younger sister and all that stuff. Oh, he also had a paper route, so his time was filled with work and school.

I planned to enjoy every moment I could because the more I enjoyed my life, it seemed the more friends were made. I could always count on Sarah and George for fun and adventures here in Decatur.

Big Brother always helped this Little Sister and we both liked our Elementary School.

CHAPTER EIGHT

Blossoming and Blossoms

"Mama, Mama, come quick! One of the boys at the Greenhouse has cut his knee!" I called out while climbing the clay bank up to our backyard. Pushing my way through the branches of the peach tree, I ran to our house.

"I'm coming," my mother called, untying her apron, and grabbing the tin of bandages and medicines that she kept handy. She had done just such as this many times before and knew just what to do.

"Tell me what happened," Mama asked as we made our way to the Greenhouse.

"Well, I didn't see, but he does have a cut," I said breathlessly.

We carefully stepped down the red-clay bank and hurried the short distance to the covered picnic shelter. This Greenhouse was where summertime arts, crafts and games took place with the neighborhood children. The McKoy Park Counselors supervised all the activities and could usually handle such emergencies, but today there were too many children. Our mother was always glad to help.

Mother gently cleaned and bandaged the boy's knee. He stopped crying and said, "Thank you, Ma'am." Then he looked up at me and gave me a big smile.

Oh Boy, my heart flipped, noticing how cute he was. Lots of us were blossoming it seemed!

Other than my starting to blossom, there were many flowering blossoms that we did enjoy. The Atlanta area was a showcase for many flowers and blooming trees, especially in the springtime. In addition to the famous Georgia Peach trees, there were Azalea bushes, Magnolias, Red Bud trees, Dogwoods, Pears, Crabapples, Mimosas, Chinaberry trees, and any number of flowering trees. Daddy had described the beauty of our yard quite well to Mama, it seemed.

Just across from our house on Adams Street our neighbors even grew magnificent big Mums in a hothouse. They sold them to the local florists to use in the corsages that were popular for the school proms. I hoped one day to be given such a corsage before going to a dance. The few times she let us walk through her greenhouse, I found it remarkable to see and smell the sweet scent of those lovely mums. There were many different colors and varieties lining the path. Everything combined to create a quiet and peaceful walk among those beauties.

There were many more types of flowering blossoms to discover, some on the way to my school. The walk from our home at one end of Spring Street to Fifth Avenue Elementary School was about five blocks, right to the other end of our street. Along the way, I would pick up flowers and leaves, and yes, sometimes boys who would join the parade to school.

As far as the actual trees and blossoms on this walk, there was a wonderful variety. We saw Crabapples with their pink flowers, Dogwoods both white and pink. I could inhale and enjoy the fragrance of Magnolias and Apple Blossoms all part of the Decatur Springtime.

The area flowers were spectacular, such as Roses, Jonquils, Irises, Pansies, Petunias, and the colorful Tulips. Mother planted bulbs of red Tulips, purple Irises and yellow Jonquils in the front yard each year. We looked forward to seeing those additions to our front yard in the Spring. She still loved to garden.

Atlanta held a Tulip Festival that displayed the pretty cupped flowers of all colors as well as other flowering bulbs. We loved to see the ladies wearing their costumes with white aprons, white starched hats and wooden shoes that made clickity clack noises on the red-bricked streets. I thought those Festivals looked like the Garden of Eden if it had Tulips with the Apple Trees.

Our yard had its own garden where Daddy would save a patch near the back of the yard to plant rows of green beans, tomatoes, cucumbers and always mint for our sweet iced tea. There were so many varieties that it would keep me busy just going around touching, smelling, and picking the various vegetables He also planted some kind of yellow flowers that helped keep bugs away. Daddy let me help him with the wire fences he made to let the beans and tomatoes climb up as they grew.

He also planted yellow squash because Mother asked him, I disliked squash, Ugh. Yet I picked it along with everything else because anything Daddy and I did together was treasured time. The garden was our time and he taught me a lot, sometimes without saying anything. Daddy was a wonderful whistler and he whistled as he worked. His pretty notes fell all around and into my ears, making me smile and the tasks go quicker.

We had four large peach trees that bore so much fruit we always had plenty for Mother to make peach cobblers, peach pies, peach preserves, and so forth. But I loved to pick a ripe fresh peach right off the tree. I would wipe the fuzz off just a little then enjoy the juicy, sweet peach while sitting under the shade of that same tree. And oh, the pink blossoms in the Spring before the peaches, were a joy to see and smell.

The family favorite for using peaches would be when Mother made a batch of the sweet sugary creamy mix for churning ice cream. We all knew exactly what to do. The boys pulled out the ice cream churn, Daddy found the bags of salt and ice he had purchased to add around the can to keep it cold and we were in business. With all of us taking turns churning it didn't take long to have ice cold creamy pink peach ice cream. Nothing was sweeter than that cold delight with the chunks of frozen peaches. Ike and Willie joined in those ice cream days by slurping up and trying to get into the bowls of that sweet stuff. They made a mess.

There was also a Pear tree plus a large Fig tree, but I avoided that fig tree. You see my older brother, Kenny, got some of the sap from the fig tree on his hand one day and became very ill. We were not sure what had happened, but he was very sick with a high fever.

The doctor discovered he had a bad allergic reaction to the sap and should always avoid figs. He was so sick it frightened all of us, especially me, because Kenny never got sick. The fact was that Kenny did not think anyone should get sick for more than one day. After that incident I avoided the figs also. Little sisters worry about big brothers.

That concern for Kenny was repaid a few years later when I came down with a bad case of pneumonia. Our family doctor was Dr. Mitchell, my friend George's father, who was very kind and caring. He came to our house to give me penicillin shots and checked on me. How we appreciated that good doctor coming to help when we were hurt or sick. That was the first time I had pneumonia, so the family was worried because I was not getting better.

I was thirteen at the time so being sick was the last thing on my mind. Then again, I was so sick that doing anything was the last thing on my mind. My friends would come and sit with me, sometimes bringing flowers. Susan Kimbrell from across the street was especially nice by reading to me or playing music on the radio to boost my spirits.

I truly appreciated their thoughtfulness during that time when I could barely open my eyes or lift my head off the pillow. I mostly slept and slept until I began to get even sicker. My fever began to spike, and I broke out in bumps all over my body.

"Mama, is Judy going to die?" Kenny implored.

With my bedroom next to the kitchen, it was easy to overhear any conversation. Some words I wished to have never heard though. *Die, what was he talking about?* Was I ever sorry I had heard that whispered comment!

I had, in fact, just experienced my own allergic reaction, to the penicillin. The doctor treated me for the symptoms, and I soon began to recover, but it was a long almost three-week ordeal. One I hoped never to repeat.

It was hard to forget the sound of deep concern in Kenny's voice. I realized he worried about his little sister just as I had about him. Our Reach family was held by a strong bond.

The blossoming blossoms of North Georgia made all of us happy, especially our Mama.

Friends, Family, Flowers, Fruits, and Fragrances along with love were cherished gifts.

CHAPTER NINE

Riding the Roads to see Roy

Roads, streets, highways, and byways seemed to cross then branch off everywhere in North Georgia. They opened new areas and new places for us to discover and did we ever do just that. There were mountains to the North and seashores to the East. Tennessee was North, Florida was to the South, and Alabama was to the West. All these were an easy drive for us to explore and enjoy.

As we worked our way through East Lake then over to the tree-lined Ponce De Leon Avenue the views became more exciting. We passed by beautiful large homes in the residential area, then it changed to the businesses, stores and more. Mother always looked to the left waiting to spot the huge Sears Roebuck Store. Everyone liked to stop there.

We kept the large Sears Catalogue right on the coffee table and flipped through it many times, especially before Christmas. In the store, Daddy and the boys always went to the tools and car parts while Mama and I enjoyed the clothing and house wares.

On the other side of the street was a dark green wooden structure holding the bleachers of the Atlanta Cracker's Baseball Stadium. Daddy would take us to the games every now and then. I loved it, plus we got to eat hot dogs and French fries. The ballgames were fun from the moment they started up that organ playing.

We continued down Ponce De Leon, heading to Atlanta. Along the way we passed the Krispy-Kreme Store. Sometimes Daddy would let us go inside to watch the doughnuts being cooked. They bumped along the conveyor belt to be covered with a hot sugary glaze. There is no fragrance that could equal the aroma wafting around us as we eagerly watched this process. Getting one of those hot, freshly made Krispy-Kreme glazed doughnuts was a treat not to be beat. We took a box of hot-off-the-rack doughnuts to give to Roy and Margie, and for us to enjoy. Yum, Heaven Indeed.

We passed various diners and eateries that held the long counters and stools. Glorious concoctions could be enjoyed of milk shakes, ice cream sodas, hamburgers, French Fries, Chili and all things delicious from the grill and soda jerk.

Our trek would continue to the finest street I had ever seen, Peachtree Street. Right there in front of us was the beautiful Fox Theater where movies were shown under a magical Sky of Stars. The huge domed top was filled with sparkling stars, so you felt as if you were seeing the night sky. As the huge grand organ played it slowly arose from below with the notes filling the entire theater. My eyes and ears had never had such magnificent sights and sounds.

From there we would pass Davidson's Department Store where we *oohed and aaahed* over the fashionable window displays. Mother loved to study these styles so she could try to recreate them with her trusty sewing machine and her sewing talent.

However, our favorite destination by far was the very popular and famous Varsity Drive-In Restaurant. The Varsity kept a rapid pace of service with one clever twist. When anyone pulled into the drive-in one of the curb-side guys or car hops would jump on the hood of the car to lead us to a place to park. He would then take our order with great flourish and humor. Those guys were fast and hilarious to watch.

We each would order our favorite like a huge hamburger with cheese and everything on it, or a foot-long hot dog with hand cut French fries and a thick milkshake or Coke. They would have all that food on a tray that hung on our rolled down car window.

This surely was an occasion of fun to share with the family, but a lot more fun in a car full of teenagers. With Georgia Tech right across from it there were usually plenty of college kids. From the time I was a pre-teen and then a full-fledged teenager, nothing tasted as delicious as those huge juicy hamburgers, crispy French fries, and thick shakes. Today we just waved as we passed by because we were nearly at Roy and Margie's place.

My thoughts wandered off to another trip we had taken even further downtown when Daddy let us come see him at his office in the State Capitol. What a magnificent building it was. I could hardly walk straight with my looking up and around, because everywhere there was something big, bright, and regal. There was so much marble, granite and brass that there seemed to be a constant echo of people moving up and down the large stairs and hallways. It was filled with beautiful sights and sounds.

Back to that day's ride, we were coming to our final stop, my brother Roy and Margie's home on the campus of Georgia Tech. I was eager to hold little Stevie once again, being the aunt and all. But Mother's eyes shone at the thought of seeing her little grandson that day.

I always enjoyed our visits with Margie, she was beautiful with a lovely singing voice and always had yummy food for us. Talking and listening to her made me happy. There were lots of bonuses to having Roy's family nearby. When the three of them came over for dinner and a visit, it was fun to take Stevie around the neighborhood to show him off and act like the best Aunt that ever was.

My brothers and I also looked forward to our visits to Roy's to see his television. He had one of the first console television sets. With his avid interest in technology, Roy just had to make one of the new television sets. It looked like our large radio we had in Waycross, but right in the middle was a circular screen about eight inches in diameter. This was a rare and magical thing to behold in this year of 1952.

Yes, the picture was small, black and white, a little fuzzy and hard to see clearly, but amazing to us.

We also were able to enjoy watching the "Rambling Wreck from Georgia Tech" parades where the students constructed all sorts of crazy vehicles. Imaginations ran wild. There were bathtubs with wheels, wheelbarrows with more wheels, barrels with wheels and so forth. They were a hoot to watch as they passed throughout the campus and looked as though they came from the junkyard. Roy loved it. Roy loved anything mechanical just as he had in Waycross tinkering on his old car.

After Stevie began to talk, he would sometimes yell in a loud voice, "Oh, Ellis." Now this sounded like a *cuss word* coming out of his sweet mouth because he said it on any occasion where he wanted to express his unhappiness. No one could figure why he so vehemently uttered that phrase *Oh, Ellis* until one day we could hear loud voices through the adjoining wall of their apartment. The next-door neighbor was quite loudly fussing at her son, her son named *Ellis*. In Stevie's little head, "Ellis, stop that, and Ellis, come here," sounded like a good thing to yell when he needed attention! And it worked. He got lots of laughs.

As Roy continued to flourish in his engineering education, he eventually landed a place in the Electrical Engineering Hall of Fame at Georgia Tech. Great things were surely ahead for he obtained a wonderful position with the Raytheon Corporation after his graduation. Here we were finally reuniting with Roy and his little family and now they were moving all the way to Massachusetts.

This branch of the Reach family was moving north and about to make their own mark on the world.

Our Reach family once more was branching out, growing, and changing.

Marjorie Barrow Reach, Stevie and Roy Wheeler Reach, Jr.

TV Shows of the '50s

Cowboy

Bonanza • Roy Rogers and Dale Evans • The Cisco Kid • The Lone Ranger • Gun Smoke • Hop Along Cassidy • Wyatt Earp • Maverick Sky King • Tales of Wells Fargo • Wagon Train • Kit Carson The Rifleman • Annie Oakley • Bat Masterson • Buffalo Bill, Jr.

Comedy and Family

Red Skelton • Jack Benny • Milton Berle • The Donna Reed Show I love Lucy • Mr. Peepers • The Honeymooners • Ozzie and Harriet Leave it to Beaver • Father Knows Best • Dr. Welby • Make Room for Daddy Dobie Gillis • Our Miss Brooks • Mr. Ed • The Real McCoy's • Superman Zorro

Game Shows

To Tell the Truth • Groucho Marx You Bet Your Life • I've Got a Secret Doctor IQ • Truth or Consequences • What's My Line • Who Do You Trust Concentration • The 64 Thousand-Dollar Question • Password

Variety and Music

American Bandstand • Dinah Shore • Andy Williams • Lawrence Welk Ed Sullivan • Pat Boone • Steve Allen • Carol Burnett • Ida Lupina Kate Smith • Arthur Godfrey's Show

Children's TV Shows

Captain Kangaroo • Kukla, Fran and Ollie • Howdy Doody • Ding Dong School • Lassie • Romper Room • Fury • Mickey Mouse Club My Friend Flicka • Mr. Wizard • Popeye's • Playhouse • Yogi Bear

Drama

Philco Theater • Alfred Hitchcock Presents • Masterpiece Theater Perry Mason • Naked City • Dragnet • Peter Gunn • Four Star Playhouse • Twilight Zone • Mr. Lucky • Make Room for Daddy Leave it to Beaver

Soap Opera

As the World Turns • The Guiding Light • Secret Storm • The Edge of Night • Brighter Day • Love of Life • Search for Tomorrow • Young Doctor Malone • General Hospital

CHAPTER TEN

The Long Arm of the Law

Our father was a Very Important Person, a true hero, not just in our own eyes, but also in those whom he had helped over the years. Yes, he was a gentle, kind, handsome, humorous, and devoted father to us. He did have an important job that seemed at odds with some of those traits.

Daddy was a *Special Investigator for the Department of Revenue in the Alcohol Tax Division*. That had to be the longest name for any position he had ever held, so I usually just said he was a Government Man. We were very proud of Daddy, he helped us, and he helped others.

In fact, it was sometimes difficult when people asked me what my father did. In the first place, I could not always say all of that correctly. Secondly, I wasn't sure what he really did every day. In the third place, people might be afraid of him. We were told to not make a big deal about his actual work. The last one was easy for me to do so I just told people he worked downtown at the Capitol Building for the Government.

Along with his impressive title he also carried a holstered gun, a badge, and sometimes a *Billy Stick* if he needed to *conk a bad guy*, ouch. He also drove a government car equipped with a siren, yes, a real siren. His car usually looked like anyone else's car, so it would not stand out like a police car, especially when doing special work. Daddy wore a suit, not a uniform now.

We used to say he worked undercover, but he would just smile his mysterious smile and shake his head. We never really knew anything for sure about Daddy's work, we just knew he seemed happy at his new position.

In Waycross he was a Revenue Agent, or Revenuer, who found illegal moonshine stills and blew them up with dynamite. We seemed to all understand blowing things up, but it was the stress of that dangerous job that caused him to have his first heart attack at age forty-six.

That was an awful time for the family since Daddy was our Daddy and he had to always be around to be our Reach Family Daddy. Then he had another smaller attack a few years later. That is what made our move to Atlanta necessary. He needed more time behind a desk and less time blowing up stills and chasing after rough and tough bootleggers and moonshiners.

During his recovery Mother had given us stern talks about keeping the household quiet and free of stress. We had all nodded our heads in genuine agreement. We heard her, we knew what she meant, but it was an impossible task. We just seemed to always do aggravating stuff like running in the house, yelling too loudly, or slamming doors.

I would shriek when Kenny and Tommy chased me, and generally cause havoc that we just did not seem capable of avoiding. Mother would get mad at us, so what would *she* do? She would *yell* at us. We thought that was funny in a way, but we always apologized to Daddy for being loud.

"Did you hear how loud Mama screamed at you, Kenny?" Even though we tried to hide our giggles behind our hands. Mother knew when she had blown a fuse. It was always our fault, after all, we were the kids.

Our respect for Daddy's job was ingrained in our lives. From the time we were small we were aware that there was danger involved with his work. After all we had seen the boxes of dynamite and the serious looking men that he met when he had to gather some information.

My brothers and I were allowed to go on some of the trips with him when he had to *meet a man*. We looked like any other family out for a car ride. He had lots of these meetings, but we knew to sit quietly in the car. The men huddled behind the car with their feet up on the bumper and their heads together, exchanging information.

There would be lots of cigar smoke, pipe smoke, cigarette smoke or chewing tobacco on display. Ugh, on the last one because it meant they had to *spit* it out after Chewing a Chaw. We could see them talk and make plans or exchange notes, or whatever secret stuff they did. We were afraid to know anything, so we just stayed quiet, but that was difficult for us to do every time.

Whenever Tommy, Kenny or I could ride along with our Dangerous Daddy, it was a special day.

Roy Wheeler Reach, Sr. As a Young Man and in Border Patrol Uniform

CHAPTER ELEVEN

A Run In with The Law Man

It wasn't long before Daddy's infamy became known throughout the area. As usual the news was met in various ways in our neighborhood. Some people would give him a polite wave, some would give him a nod then scurry away quickly, others would ask him all sorts of questions. Naturally if there was any trouble the Law Man could always be asked to help. He also could and would assist in preparing anyone's taxes, if asked.

The neighborhood kids seemed surprised, delighted, full of fear, and even a bit of awe about our Daddy's position. It was not long before some of those local boys came face to face with my father, much to their dread. This incident just happened to involve a boy I knew.

My best friend at school was George Mitchell, as I probably have already mentioned many times. One of his best buddies was Bartley Snead who lived just around the corner from us. He and a friend had an unfortunate run-in-with-the-law experience.

Even though people in the area knew Daddy was in law enforcement many were not sure in what capacity. They did know, however, that his car had a siren and that he carried a gun. That was enough to merit him a lot of respect.

One day Bartley and another buddy of his were playing in the park just behind the clay bank at the back of our yard. There was an iron grate in the ground near the skating rink that covered a big hole. That mysterious hole had intrigued a lot of boys and some girls, like me. This curious obstacle created a lot of attention. All the kids in the neighborhood wanted to know just how deep that hole was below the heavy grate.

Well, those two boys started throwing rocks into the hole to see if that would tell the depth. Those few rocks proved unsatisfactory to quell their nine-year-old curiosity. More rocks were needed, many more rocks in fact.

Now those two boys were so fully caught up in their quest that they started frantically looking for any rocks of any size anywhere they could find them. They came upon our backyard bank and spotted a bunch of nice big stones. Some were pressed into the red clay, and some were easier to pull out than others. Their eyes lit up in anticipation.

Incidentally, those rocks and stones had been carefully placed there to keep the bank from eroding or collapsing. That never entered their boy brains as they rapidly began plucking the rocks out, paying no attention to anything around them. They were on a quest, right?

When they finally paused to take a breath, they happened to look up. Both were struck still with fear. The Law Man was standing on the top of the bank above them. His hands were firmly on his hips and there was a stern look on his face as he glared down at the miscreants. The two boys were still tightly clutching those big rocks. This was bad.

Then the Arm of the Law said, "What are you boys getting into down there?"

Neither one of them said anything. Where were their voices? Where was his gun?

The Law continued, "This is private property, and you are damaging our yard by pulling out those stones." Then that Law Man asked the dreaded question, "What are your names and addresses?"

Names and addresses? The boys looked at one another. Did they have names, or did they live anywhere?

My father finished his reproach to the boys with the words that no child ever wanted to hear, "I need to let your parents know what you boys are up to in our yard."

Poor Bartley, he truly was a sweet little guy. He also was the son of a Baptist Preacher. Could this day get any worse or be any more frightening for him?

What if *The Law Man* did pull out his gun, or maybe that scary Billy Stick, then what would they do?

He and his buddy did what any God-fearing and parent-fearing boys would do in such a dire situation; they dropped the rocks and tore home. Lickety-split, those two were out of there.

Bartley ran to his bedroom, jumped on his bed, pulled his knees up to his chin and gripped his legs. Maybe he could make himself disappear if he pushed himself way into the corner of the bed.

He waited and waited for that fateful call to come. He never had uttered one word about his run in with the law. No call came that day. No call came the next day, or that whole week.

Whew! He was out of the woods and could once again relax and show his face around the neighborhood.

`Wrong. The next day, sure enough, his parents got the call. The incident had pretty much lost some of its urgency at that point. Bartley had no idea of this situation, however. He had watched his life pass before his eyes for several days.

He and his buddy managed to get off with just the stern warning, "Be careful to never damage or trespass on anyone's property." Perhaps some such reproach.

Unfortunately, Bartley moved to Atlanta the next year, so I did not get to know him well. I am sure he did not wish to meet my Daddy. again. The sad thing is he never got to know what a kind and gentle man my father truly was.

That is why it took Daddy so long to make that call to the boys' parents. In fact, it was Mother who had the final say. She convinced him the boys needed to learn a lesson, so he finally did make the call.

The punishment had to fit the crime. That call allowed both sets of parents to handle their sons as each saw fit. It had been so long after the incident when that call finally came, their parents let them off lightly.

However, none of us ever wanted Daddy to be mad at us. Usually, it was Mother who gave us her hands-on punishment. The worst situation was if Mother did nothing after a bad infringement of a family law.

In that situation she could blow her stack, so she chose to say these words, "You just wait until your father gets home from work. I will give him an earful about what you have done."

Then she usually added a hex, "You're going to get a good licking."

The wrongdoer was usually very quiet and watched the clock to see when Daddy would be home. Tick-tock, tick-tock. Daddy would barely get a foot in the door of the kitchen, before he would be barraged with a litany of awful deeds that had been done that day, ending with, "I just could not manage the situation. Roy, you are going to have to deal with this. Frankly, I have had enough."

Poor Daddy had to be thrust into the middle of a mess again without knowing the whole situation. He shook his head, removed his leather belt, and called the offender outside.

"I have to give you a few licks so you won't make your mother upset like this again," he would say through clenched teeth.

Yeah, it was Mother's wrath that we all feared, and the consequences.

CHAPTER TWELVE

Christmas with the Tin Man

Merry Christmas! This was the first year celebrating in our Decatur home. The weather was chilly and crisp, perfect. Could there be snow? In Waycross we had tromped out to the woods to cut the perfect tree, but this year we had to do things differently, no woods were close by us. Mama had been seeing the new aluminum trees that were being shown in the magazines and stores and decided we needed to go modern.

The silver shiny tree was unboxed, sorted, and assembled after a lot of hits and misses. Now it was up in the living room ready for decorating.

Before starting the tree trimming, Kenny and Tommy sprayed our big picture window with a white, snowy *Merry Christmas*, beautiful. Writing regularly was hard enough for me but writing backwards would be impossible. They never asked me to help with that greeting, smart.

After digging out our beloved glass ornaments from the attic, we were ready to adorn those stiff tree limbs. We had always finished our trees with lots of tinsel, and we would with the silver tree, more silver. Daddy had first strung our big colorful lights on the tree since he could do that job so well. After the ornaments were hung and the tinsel carefully placed, the finishing touch was the top ornament. Befitting of this aluminum tree, a strange silver blue spire tree topper had been chosen by Mama, not our big star.

We all stepped back to view the finished shimmering tree and none of us said a word. Instead of our usual live tree, with the wonderful pine or fir scent, we were all smelling *nothing*. The more I looked at the spectacle, I had images of the *Tin Man* from *The Wizard of Oz* who only wanted a heart. There he was with lights on his tin arms and tin legs lit up in red, yellow, green and blue lights. That strange tin spire sat atop his head instead of a funnel. The tinsel gave him a quivering look as if the big *Tin Man Tree* would walk towards us by himself. It was a bit scary, maybe just to me.

Then looking at Mother, we saw a contented smile of pure love for this creation. We looked at one another, shrugged our shoulders and said how wonderful it was. We loved our Mama and really liked seeing her that happy with her hands clasped under her smiling face.

Then she rushed into the kitchen and brought out the bowls of oranges, apples, date, and nuts in their shells with a nutcracker. All these blended together into a sweet fruity treat for our senses. Now we all smiled because the Christmas spirit was in the Reach household. We were ready for Christmas morning.

Christmas Eve was a restless night for me because I had worried when we moved up here about there being no chimney. In Waycross Santa had a choice between two chimneys that he could come down to deliver our toys and goodies. What would happen this Christmas? Being the youngest of five children, I had been told many stories about Jolly Old Saint Nicholas that kept the dream alive for me.

This year I was turning nine and had been wanting to keep that magical feeling in my heart, but something kept nagging at my young brain. The actual delivery of all those toys after being piled into a big red sleigh driven by flying reindeer was really bothering me. Maybe I will sneak a peek into the off limits living to see myself if *He* is there.

That Christmas Eve I listened at the closed door and could hear strange rustling sounds and bells. What was that all about? Whatever it was had scared me so much that I ran, jumped into my bed and covered myself with the blanket. Tonight, was not the time to make a fuss; I would do as I was told and worry about that Santa thing next year. I slept.

The morning of Christmas was always very exciting, but we knew the rules. We had to eat breakfast first. I kept looking at that swinging door leading into the dining and living rooms. Come on can we go now? And finally, the door was opened, and the sweet smell of Christmas wafted all around us.

The tinsel covered silver Tin Man Tree was aglow and shimmering, it looked prettier this morning and not so scary. We each headed to our own chair full of all sorts of stuff, but we first dove into the stockings. They always held the same thing each year, we loved it all. The yummy Lifesavers Book, red candy canes, gum drops, Cracker Jacks, a can of popcorn, packs of chewing gum and bubble gum, nuts and fruit. Always on top were rolls of caps for our pop guns, firecrackers, and sparklers for New Year's Eve. On our chair was a box of chocolate covered cherries and a box of chocolate drops. Man, this was all super neat.

And look, I got what I was hoping for, the pretty jewelry music box with a little dancing ballet dancer, even a key to keep my treasures safe, whatever those would be. There were new roller skates, coloring books with a giant box of Crayola's, a new jump rope, a Slinky, and a set of Dominoes. My mouth was going to break from smiling so big. Kenny and Tommy were evidently having fun too because I heard happy sounds from them like *geeze, cool, nice, man* and so forth.

I smiled at Mama and Daddy who were at the edge of their seats watching our expressions and shrieks of joy. They reached under the tree to hand out the pretty wrapped gifts from Patsy, Roy, Granny, Aunt Helen, and others. As I watched them it seemed as if that *Tin Man Tree* had moved forward just a bit. My imagination was working overtime, but Boy Howdy it looked as if it was inching forward.

I shook my head to clear those nutty thoughts. Mama was urging me to take the pretty wrapped gift from Patsy. I quickly unwrapped the box to see a pink silk neck scarf, little Poodle scatter pins, and even bangle bracelets. *Golly Gee Whiz, such grown up gifts!*

Mother then opened another gift with a beautifully flowered silk scarf and pair of pale blue gloves from her brother, our Uncle George. Then I saw her eyes glisten with tears as she opened Daddy's gift, a double-stranded pearl necklace and matching pearl clip earrings. He put his arms around her, then she turned to give him a big hug. Daddy did good for Mama that Christmas. Mother gave Daddy a handsome new bathrobe and pajamas. I think he was a bit embarrassed opening these rather private gifts, but he gave her one of his big smiles. We all were having a great time sharing this morning together.

Christmas was a glorious, delicious, fun time filled with the joy and happiness our parents had given us. After we picked up the Living Room a bit, Mother began singing, filling the room with *Joy to the World*, *Oh Holy Night*, *Away in a Manger, and Silent Night*. The rest of us joined her in singing those glorious Christmas Carols like *Jingle Bells* in sweet harmony.

Yes, there were gifts, toys, candy, and goodies, but we each knew the true meaning of Christmas. I had turned nine the week before and seemed to feel a stronger sense of that belief as we sang and joyfully gave thanks.

Christmas afternoon was filled with telephone calls to and from family and friends. I could hardly wait to get together with my friends to try out my wonderful new toys. We had our delicious Christmas Supper together of baked ham, sweet potatoes, and scalloped potatoes ending with Mama's homemade fruit cake.

Merry Christmas and have a Happy New Year for 1953!

Sweets and Snacks in the '50s

Milk Duds • Sugar Daddy • Sugar Babies • Assorted Hard Candy
Jaw Breakers • Bazooka Bubblegum • Fizzies • Chunky chocolate
Butterfingers • Baby Ruth • Snickers • Almond Joy • Mounds Tootsie
Roll • Pay Day • Charms • All Day Sucker • Boston Peanuts Chocolate
Raisins • Milky Way • Junior Mint • Hershey Bar • Red Hots
Bit-o-Honey • Jujubes • Dumdums • M&Ms • Necco Wafers • Licorice
Whopper • Malted balls • Lifesavers • O-Henry Bar • Chewing gum
Bazooka BubbleGum • Taffy

Novelty Candy

Candy Cigarettes • Red Wax Lips • Wax Teeth • Wax Bottles • Candy
Bracelet Beads • Maryjane's • Baseball Card Bubblegum • Pixie Stix
Chic-o-Stix • Taffy • Valentine Hearts • Red Hots • Coconut Bars
Red Peppermint • Sticks and Canes • Atomic Fireballs • Various
Marshmallow Treats • Such as Peanuts, Chick's • Chocolate Eggs Bunnies
Blo-Pops • B-Bats • All-Day Suckers

After School Snacks

Potato Chips • Fritos • BBQ Potato Chips • Popcorn • Peanuts
Saltine or Ritz Crackers with Peanut butter • Cookies • Boiled peanuts
Roasted in Shell Peanuts • Toasted Pecans • Chocolate or Caramel Fudge
Bosco in Milk • Kool-Ade • Malted Milk • Any Good Leftovers in
the Frigidaire!

Party Food

Pigs-in-a-Blanket • Swedish meatballs • Chips & Onion Dip • Fruit
Kebabs • Stuffed Mushrooms • Finger Sandwiches • Celery with Cream
or Pimento Cheese • Ritz Crackers with Cheese and Olive • Homemade
Cookies • Donuts • Cakes • Caramel or Chocolate Fudge • Ambrosia
Deluxe Nuts

CHAPTER THIRTEEN

The Great Bonfire of '53

My friends and I were glad to be going back to school after our Christmas break so we could see one another. George, Bartley, Neil, Shay and I gathered for our walk wearing jackets, hats and mittens. January of 1953 was shivery cold. We gathered and giggled about our Christmas Day sharing the times with excitement as Neal, Larry, Betty, Linda, Cynthia, and others joined us.

The walk to Fifth Avenue School was extra fun that day as we chattered, because in front of many houses there were dried Christmas trees waiting to be removed. Many were glistening as the sunlight bounced off the silver shimmering tinsel still left on some trees. We laughed seeing tinsel thrown in globs among the branches. It was hard to keep those thin strips straight for the next year. That meant last year's impatience left knots for this year. Many people ran to the store to get new boxes to ease the frustration. We thought it was funny.

Looking back, I saw George and Bartley with their heads together, excitedly planning some new adventure no doubt. They were waving their arms, pointing back to George's house, and nodding their heads. Evidently their big plan was going to come to fruition. Oh dear, what were they going to do next? Who could know, as they chose to not share their new ploy with us?

Well, George's brain had started working overtime that day on a plan to use those used-up trees. The two of them decided to collect the trees left at the curbs. On the surface it seemed like a nice gesture on their part. They would clear away the now dead and dried up Christmas trees from the front of their neighbor's yards to make everything look neat and tidy.

How thoughtful and sweet those boys were, or were they? Well, there was always an ulterior motive to their projects. Yes, that did seem to be a considerate gesture on the part of those two perfectly mannered little guys. Oh, they did remove the trees from people's yard, but just what did they have in mind for themselves?

One thing I knew for sure, our Silver Tin Man Tree would not be out by the curb, not this year. He was boxed up and stored in our attic with the Christmas ornaments, probably still looking for a heart and his funnel hat. They all giggled at my description of our tree.

The two boys later took as many of those dried pines and firs that they could drag and began to pile them on top of one another, over and over. The wobbly stack grew quite large and ungainly, but it should be safe, or so the two boys thought. After all they used a ladder to pile them carefully way in the back of George's yard, away from harm.

"Look at that huge pile of trees we made, now let's light the fire!" Bartley and George exclaimed proudly, "Hey, let's see how big the fire would get if we stacked them even higher. No, let's just light this match now and watch."

It didn't take much of a spark from one match to catch those dried trees into a blistering blaze. They were immensely proud of their deed. The once beautifully decorated and adorned Christmas trees now were an impressive fire that sparked, popped, and blazed high into the sky.

The dark smoke from that pyre began to cover the neighborhood. The neighbors stuck their heads out of their doors and realized the blaze came from the Mitchell's house. They knew what a responsible family they were, and Dr. Mitchell surely had it well in hand.

"Oh, and look it's that nice, well-behaved Mitchell boy and his friend the Preacher's son, Bartley." All would be fine they thought.

They did indeed keep their watchful eyes on that fire. They got very hot themselves while standing watch beside that inferno. Those four eyes got bigger and started to sting their already red-hot faces as the flames grew higher. The two ambitious boys were quite fortunate on that exact day because there was not a hint of wind or even a breeze. That was lucky for them.

Being the good young boys they were, George and Bartley had completed their project and there were, surprisingly, no ill consequences. Boys did love fires. They shared a great Christmas Bonfire in 1953.

Now George was smart and all, but he did have a few little odd hobbies, many of them he shared with me. The main one being collecting live snakes. Well, since he was such a nice boy and cute, I let him teach me how to catch and hold a few snakes.

Then he showed me how to hold many more snakes such as the green garter or garden snakes, plus other reptiles like lizards, and the like. He showed me how to hold them just behind their head with one hand, while draping their long body over my other hand. Thankfully, he also taught me how to distinguish the good from the bad varieties of reptile, and when to approach or stay away.

I learned that snakes were not slimy creatures, but in reality, quite smooth feeling. Gradually I grew to like the feel of their cool skins and watched with fascination when they would shed those skins.

George did not stop at snakes though. He taught me how to capture spiders, grasshoppers, lizards, frogs, toads, and worms. We put them into jars with holes poked into the lids. Each little glass container had the correct environment for each critter, some with grass and some had bugs, and all had a little water.

George was inquisitive and enjoyed observing the little critters and I did too. When any of them looked like they were in distress I wanted immediately to let them go free. George gave me one of his pursed mouth looks and a frown, but he usually relented. We would unscrew the top and release the creatures to freedom. Some barely moved along, but most critters gained their freedom.

Bartley already knew these things because boys just knew this stuff. But there was no way I was going to enter any of their conflagration projects in the future. Nope George and Bartley can enjoy that pastime all by themselves.

Creepy Crawlies

I got over the willies after catching some lizards at last.

The toads were too fat, and the grasshoppers were too fast.

The spiders were creepy, and the worms were slippery.

Some were wobbly and slow, some of them were just ickey.

It was all good when we were on George's terms.

We only lost two spiders, one lizard, and two worms.

But George said their lifespans were not very long.

So, I just decided to trust him as we went along!

CHAPTER FOURTEEN

Big Sister Is Finally Home

Patience, yes, I had looked that word up in the dictionary just to be sure what it meant. Mother had told me I needed to have that often enough and it did mean to have the *ability to wait*. Mama was always right. Patience paid off and my sister would soon arrive to be back doing stuff with our family just like it had been in Waycross.

Waiting on the front steps of our house for what seemed an eternity for her to arrive, at last I saw Daddy's car turn into the driveway. There she was, Patsy began waving out of the window when she spotted me.

"Hey, there Baby Sister!" She called out and smiled. "Look how much you have grown you pretty girl!"

She was here, Patsy was home. I felt like my world was right again and our home at 16 Spring Street was also a complete home just as it should be. I relaxed a little at that moment, I think because everything felt right. Yes, sure enough patience paid off and all would be well.

After big hugs I said, "Patsy, I was worried you were not going to come up here to Decatur. I thought you would stay in Waycross forever."

"Oh, Judy, you are a mess. I wanted to be with the family a little longer and thought you needed your old roommate," saying this she gave me another great big hug.

As we walked up the steps and into our new home, it was great to show it to Patsy. I asked her when she would start working for Mr. Rich at the big Rich's Department store in Atlanta.

"They need me to start next Monday. It was exciting to be through with Mercer University and working in Waycross, and now I have this new position," she expressed this to me with her usual warm smile.

"Yeah, maybe Mama and I can visit you at your office sometimes."

"After I am settled in there, we will plan that," she said patting my hand reassuringly.

Mother joined us and gave Patsy a hug with a smile. She was pleased to have Patsy here with the rest of us at last. Daddy came in carrying two of Patsy's suitcases. I grabbed her hand to show her the bedroom. Daddy followed us, putting her luggage down, then went back out for the rest of her things.

She began unpacking while I helped her get some hangers. We had cleared out a whole dresser for her and I had moved a lot of my things into my dressing table for now. Those poor little drawers were stuffed tight. It did not matter one bit. We would figure it all out later. I was content. This was a happy day for all of us. Kenny and Tommy would be home soon so we can have the supper mother had prepared.

Patsy turned and asked, "Is that fried chicken I smell? Yummy, I have missed your cooking, Mama." Boy Howdy, that made our mother smile. The Reaches would enjoy a home-made meal together as a family, all was right with the world.

Patsy had always been a giving person and generous to our entire family. After she began her position as an Executive Secretary, she wanted to help with the family financially. She knew that Daddy was a proud man and very careful with money, so he would not want her to give him anything. In fact, our Daddy was the one who would always be there to help a relative if they needed a little money here or there.

"Daddy, I am grown up now and should pay some rent to show you I am a responsible person." Patsy spoke these words so softly that no one could hear his or her conversation. She was well aware of Daddy's pride and how seriously he took his role as the Bread Winner and Head of this Family.

I tried to listen behind closed doors to understand all this. Frankly I did not know what anybody was talking about. Even if I heard everything, I would have to ask somebody what they meant. Then these thoughts kept popping into my head.

"You don't have to pay to live in your family home, do you? Was I supposed to be paying? What was rent anyway?" Evidently, I would never find out such answers.

Then it occurred to me that I was getting 25 cents for doing chores, so *they* were paying *me*. However, I was not going to say anything about that particular arrangement. I think I'll worry about that rent thing later.

My cagey sister was stubborn and clever, so she devised various ways of paying Daddy with a little money here or there. The finest plan she had was the time she sent Daddy a letter from Rich's Department Store announcing he had won a prize of Fifty Dollars.

Daddy read it and immediately pulled out his well-worn, black Underwood typewriter and quickly tapped out a reply. His method of typing was to use only his two forefingers braced with his thumbs. Those fingers would fly across the keys with amazing speed.

The following is a copy of that exact letter of reply. This is just one small example of Daddy's wit and intelligence as well as a tribute to his feelings for his daughter, priceless.

Roy W. Reach

16 Spring Streets

Decatur, Georgia

July 23, 1954

Miss Patsy Reach

c/o Rich's Inc.

Atlanta, Georgia

Dear Miss Reach:

I have your letter of July 21, and check in the amount of $50.00 which was awarded to me for having the youngest Secretary at Rich's Inc. I am honored by this distinction and appreciate the $50.00 prize. In connection with the above contest, I am happy to announce that I was runner-up in a recent contest as "Being the only bay-windowed father in DeKalb County who sits in his back yard nursing a duck, who has a "woman" who talks with clenched teeth; a 16-year-old son who rushes off at 8:30 AM five days a week to be a counselor at the YMCA with seven and eight-year-old boys; a fourteen-year-old boy who each week knocks on neighbor's doors and asks for money for his paper route; a 10-year-old girl who dresses in frills and ribbons on Sundays then catches snakes etc. on week days; a 22-year-old daughter who judges unusual contests, then pays the awards personally; and lastly a duck that cheeps like a sparrow, walks like a rhinoceros, eats dog food, and sits on eggs under a chicken house.

Thanking you again for the above award.

Fatherly yours,

Roy W. Reach, Esq.

Patsy's being home was making everyone more relaxed and happier, it seemed. I know Mama had worried about Patsy while she away at college and work. Now she could relax and enjoy her family again. Mother and Daddy used this time to spend the day together a few times on the weekend while Patsy was there to be in charge.

Having watched Mother cook for quite a while, I had begun to try some recipes on my own. I made all types of cookies and even cakes, but by far my favorite treat to make was fudge. I could whip up a batch of chocolate fudge with pecans, caramel fudge, and even divinity candy. Divinity was definitely not my divine specialty.

This stemmed from the disastrous day my sister Patsy decided to make some divinity candy while she was watching us. Mother and Daddy were away for the day. That recipe required pouring a hot sugar-syrup mixture into beating egg whites.

Well, we had a state-of-the-art Kitchen Aid mixer with a glass bowl, so this is what was used for the divinity recipe. As Patsy began to slowly pour the syrup into the furiously beating egg whites, Kenny, Tommy and I looked on expectantly. Well, evidently the syrup was just a little too hot or Patsy poured a little too fast, because the next sound we heard was a *Big Pop*, like a gunshot.

The glass bowl starting to crack, then to break, finally the whole bowl shattered. At the same time the beaters were furiously spinning, flinging white, hot, sticky syrup all over the kitchen. It went onto the counter, spilled onto the floor, and even spewed onto the ceiling. Oh No, now what? Looking at each other and being grateful our parents were not there to see that mess, we all pitched in and cleaned off the sticky goop before it became permanent glue.

We had quite a family bond, and Patsy managed to buy a replacement bowl for the mixer. It was a very dramatic and messy day. From that point I started only making chocolate or caramel fudge. Divinity candy was good, but it was not worth the price.

Big sister being home made all the Reach Family happy, especially me.

CHAPTER FIFTEEN

The Reach's at Rich's

"Can we ride the trolley downtown today to see Patsy at Rich's?" I asked my mother.

"Well, I do need to pick up some fabric and patterns for a new dress for you to wear to church. Why don't you put on something pretty and I will change into a nice dress also," Mama said.

She always made sure we were well dressed for any trip to Atlanta. Going downtown was special and meant looking your best, maybe even donning gloves and hats. It was wonderful and gave me one more chance to dress up in pretty clothes.

Trolleys were things of wonder to me. They made their way so easily throughout the Atlanta area while attached to overhead cables. They clanked, popped, and whirred as they ran along on their assigned route. Waycross surely never held anything this mysterious, so anytime we could ride a trolley car it was exciting.

One transfer was required then a short walk to reach the entrance to Rich's Department Store. On the way we would go by one of my favorite places, the Planter's Peanut Store. There was the tall Peanut Man propped by the door sporting a monocle, black cane, and top hat. He was cute and always made me smile. Seeing a sophisticated peanut with a hat and cane was funny.

This store happened to be one of the first to install doors that opened automatically. It was not only a treat to watch the doors open magically, but we were greeted with the rush of the cool air conditioning followed by the heavenly fragrance of roasted peanuts, cashews, and pecans. It was a sweet shock to my senses.

"Mama, can we go inside? It smells good, doesn't it?" This was an easy request, as Mother would always like to go through those electric doors to feel the coolness inside. The aroma alone was very enticing.

We would each get a small, crisp paper bag filled with some freshly prepared salted peanuts. Delicious! But we had more things to do and more places to be.

"Thank you, Ma'am," I held her hand as I smiled up at her.

"You are welcome, Honey. I like that store also," she added.

We had reached our destination, Rich's Department Store in Downtown Atlanta. There were two different parts of this large store, one side held the Fashion Store and the other side the Home Store. They were connected by glassed walkways over the street on very floor but the main floor. It was exciting and a thrill to look down and see the traffic going under and people crossing over the street.

During Christmas each floor was decorated and lit up, sometimes having different local choirs singing on each level. It was a magnificent sight to see as we drove toward and under the walkways. One huge tree stood at the very top of the building. The fun Pink Pig ride at Christmas was something children and *big children* waited for each year. It was a big Pink elevated train winding around and through the decorated Store. Santa Clause waited for the kiddies to tell him what gifts they hoped to receive. Rich's Department store made the holidays come alive for everyone lucky enough to enjoy a visit there.

We reached our destination and began working our way toward Patsy. The Home Store is where Mr. Rich was and where Patsy's office was also located. This was the reason we began the shopping trip in that section. I was about to bust at the seams to see where her office was.

Patsy had studied hard to achieve her secretarial position. I knew that because she had been away while she attended Business School and then Mercer University. She was smart all right. When I learned that she was going to work at my favorite store in the whole world, I had been thrilled. Then she said she was working for one of the big bosses and I nearly flipped.

There she was looking smart and efficient as she went about her duties. As always, she looked super and was perfectly dressed. Patsy was petite and looked wonderful in everything to me. Today she wore a dark brown skirt and matching sweater with a single strand of pearls and little pearl drop earrings. Her light brown hair was short in soft curls around her pretty face and hazel eyes, all framing her ever-present smile. My big sister was beautiful.

Spotting us, she waved her hand for us to come into the office. We didn't hug her to embarrass her while she was working. When her boss came into her office, she quickly stood up to introduce everyone.

"Mr. Rich, I would like you to meet my mother Libby Reach and my sister Judy," she politely stated.

He was a handsome man wearing a fancy dark suit with a maroon tie. He even had a little maroon handkerchief peeking out of his breast pocket. He had a gold tie clip and gold cuff links in the cuffs of his starched shirt, just showing from his suit coat. He was impressive and made me nervous.

Then he nodded his head and reached out his hand to Mother. She lightly held it for a small shake. Then he said, "It is so nice to meet you and may I say how good it is to have your daughter working here."

Mr. Rich spoke to her with a slight bow, "She is bright and a pleasure to be around. She also is fitting into the routine of everything quickly."

"Why that is nice to hear, and we both are glad to meet you." Looking over at Patsy with a proud smile Mother continued, "We are all very proud of Patsy and I am pleased to be able to see where my daughter is working."

Mother then added with just a trace of nervousness in her voice, "This is such a lovely store."

Meanwhile my eyes had gotten too big for my face and the lump in my throat was about to blow out of my neck. I could not move. Something on that floor must have made me feel stuck or something, it was weird.

"This is my sister, Judy, Mr. Rich. She has been wanting to meet you," Patsy added with a smile as they both looked at me.

Of course, they both looked at me. Why did she say that? Now they were both looking at me.

"My you are a pretty young lady. It is nice to meet you also," the big handsome man said. Then he reached his hand out to me.

I looked at it as if was a lobster's claw, what was I supposed to do now? I was struck dead still.

"Judy, shake Mr. Rich's hand," Mama said trying to stun me out of my trance with a little shake of my shoulders.

My hand flew out so fast I nearly hit his arm, but he very nicely took my hand. After he had given me a small handshake and a big smile, I managed to smile back and stop shaking. My eyes had returned to their normal size and the lump in my throat settled down so I could now swallow. But could I speak yet?

"Judy is my roommate at home." Patsy quickly added. "We share a bedroom which is now furnished with the handsome gray bedroom suite I bought from the store."

That happy reminder snapped me awake, "Yes, sir, it is the most beautiful furniture I have ever seen in my entire life. It has a padded bench seat and a big round mirror over the dresser and a tall chest and a big double bed, oh, and two bedside tables."

Man, when my voice came back it came back too fast; I stopped as my face turned red.

With a small laugh Patsy added, "Judy is a fan of Rich's and obviously a fan of Rich's furniture" Then she gave me a reassuring hug and a light kiss on my cheek.

I smiled; I was going to live.

"Mrs. Reach, you have two lovely daughters. Patsy is a very capable and efficient secretary. We are proud to have her working here," he politely said.

Mother smiled at Patsy and me, obviously with pride. Once Mr. Rich left, I relaxed and so did Patsy and Mama. Patsy took my hand and introduced us to her office friends. My older sister could always make me smile. She had the gift of making me feel special and loved.

Over a period of time, as our shopping trips downtown continued, I became quite proficient at knowing the layout of the whole department store. We could be in any part of Rich's, and I would know exactly which floor, which elevator, and which department we needed to reach. It was my own department store.

Those trips with Mother became rarer as I grew up and gained more friends. Then the outings turned into adventures, giving me a feeling of independence. My friends and I would make the trolley trip just by ourselves, transfer included. We all made sure we were dressed just right and used our best manners.

When we passed by Mr. Peanut, I did get a tug at my heart. Especially when that aroma of those freshly cooked nuts of every sort wafted out, if the doors happened to open as we passed."

Since I knew the layout of Rich's so well, we could easily navigate the store to know exactly where we needed to be. Knowing Patsy was working at Rich's was always fun for me tell my friends. While in that big store we would pass the fancy Magnolia Room Restaurant, the Tearoom, and then the Bakery as we made our way throughout every floor.

We would talk of how wonderful it would be to have the store all to ourselves for one day just to explore and enjoy. We did more looking than spending though. A little purchase here and there perhaps.

Sometimes at home while the family waited for Patsy to return from work, we might see her carrying something special. We knew that pastel box tied with string would hold a treat she had purchased from the Rich's Bakery. By far my favorite was the exotic Hawaiian cake filled with coconut, pineapple, and cherries, yum, life was good!

Our Reach's Life was Richer with Rich's

CHAPTER SIXTEEN

The McKoy Park Pipe Adventure

"Hey Judy, come see what I found over there in McKoy Park," my friend George was calling out to me while I was in the back yard picking some peaches off one of our trees.

Smiling, I waved at him as he came nearer. He had a big grin on his face and had run so quickly he was out of breath. George was my buddy and yes, my boyfriend, so when he said he found something, you bet I had to see what it was. He always had something interesting going on, and I usually wanted to know what it was. I needed to hear any new trouble he was going to get into so I could maybe help out or something.

He climbed up the clay bank to our yard then I held out a peach for him. He took it of course, then took a big juicy bite. I laughed seeing the juice running down his shirt, then I took a bite of mine. He pointed at me, and we both laughed. Yes, I had peach juice on my pink top. We had an easy friendship.

"Tell me what you found," I was very interested, naturally.

"Yeah, over there, that big heavy grate covers a deep hole," He pointed with excitement in his voice as if he had unearthed a treasure, or at least the big hole that held that treasure.

"Oh, I know that place. Carol Kelly and I roller skate on that paved rink near it, so we have looked down there with curiosity too," I told him, trying to match his excitement, but not quite understanding yet what the big deal was.

"Yes, yes, but that grate protects a big pipe, don't you see?" My blank look showed him I was not excited about his great revelation. It was a deep hole and a big pipe. But I went down the bank of our yard to run with him over to the mysterious and magical pipe he had unearthed.

He was already standing on the big grate excitedly pointing down. "OK, let me see that pot of gold you have found down there," I said with a laugh.

He knew I was kidding him.

We both knelt to check it out and sure enough you could see the opening to a large cement culvert I had never noticed. Well, I never really was interested in studying a deep hole when there was roller skating to enjoy nearby.

"Oh no, George, this is the very same trouble-causing grate your friend Bartley messed with, remember?" I was now a little worried. "Oh, my Daddy got mad at him and his buddy for pulling big rocks out of our clay bank to toss down this hole."

"Shoot yeah, I heard all about it and thought it was hilarious," he laughingly replied. See, boys always stick together when there's trouble.

"He didn't know then that clay bank was part of your yard. You can bet Bartley knows it well now."

I just looked at George and shook my head. He was still laughing about poor Bartley's brush with the Law Man. "Boy Howdy, your Daddy scared the *bejeepers* out of those two," he said shaking his head.

He was getting way too much pleasure out of that nice Bartley's misadventure. "You know, Mister George, that could have been you getting into trouble, he is your good friend after all."

"Well, what do you have in his mind for us to do with this grate thing? I mean, do you really have a plan?" I asked, now with my curiosity in full swing.

"Yeah, I think I know what we can do. You can see how all those rocks people have tossed in has made it easier to climb down there," George stated this as if it would now be a snap to get down into that hole.

Was that supposed to explain everything? Climb down there? He wanted to climb into that hole? Was he nuts? But I managed to ask in a cool voice, "And just exactly how do you intend to get that heavy grate moved so we could even try to climb down?" Yep, that would put a stop to this madness.

"I have already figured that out, trust me," George said calmly. Of course, why he probably would have made detailed drawings of his plan already. I think by now we knew George was a clever and smart boy.

He had picked up a three-foot long pipe and was now holding it as if it was a prized turkey. Guess I was supposed to react as if this was the perfect solution. "Look," he explained. "We use it for leverage to move the grate."

"Leverage?" I asked, "You mean use it as a lever to move it sort of like a jack for a car?"

Yeah, I was smart too, but acted like a girl sometimes. Now was not the time to act like a girlie ten-year-old, even though I was just that most of the time.

Then George gave me one of his big old grins like he was proud of me. That's why we were friends.

Together we got the pipe under the grate just enough to be able to push it aside. We were not very big so we could squeeze through a small opening. Yes, George was just so doggone cute that I followed him."

He told me that the large culvert must come out somewhere on the other side of the baseball field.

"The baseball field, are you kidding me? Look how far that is from here." I was getting worked up at this point, "George Mitchell, you intend for us to walk all the way through that culvert underneath the ballpark to the other end? Are you out of your mind?"

"Well sure, what else would we do? Come on let's explore this before we do anything else," George declared.

Never wanting to act like a *scaredy cat* in front of him, I bravely said, "OK, let's do that first because it seems pretty creepy. It takes a long pipe to cover that distance. It's got to be dark in the middle too, real dark." Skepticism was creeping into my good senses.

We climbed up and worked our way out of the culvert. We knew what we had to do. After looking at each other with knowing glances, we streaked across the oval skating rink. We slid down the bank to the ball field and ran across to the other side of the park.

There it was, almost hidden in the brush, another large opening just like the opening to the culvert on the other end. A small trickle of water was dripping out of it and slowly moving into the stream in the woods. We both were well acquainted with this particular stream. It meandered through this wooded area and joined a bigger stream that worked its way throughout the neighboring woods.

"Neat-O!" I yelled, like now it was all going to be OK. We had made a discovery about our very own woods we knew so well. We *thought* we knew so well, that is. Exploring was fun.

"Well, do you want to check out the whole pipe?" George asked me with a look that meant "Please, let's see what it is like in there."

"Sure," I replied, with an unrealistic trust in his scheme, "But let's get a flashlight and some food, okay?" We did just that and then began warily carrying out our very scary journey. After making some Bologna and cheese sandwiches, we found a flashlight. *Daddy would not be happy about this,* I thought.

We were now on our way to the Big Pipe Adventure of McKoy Park. We dropped the flashlight and the bag of sandwiches down first. Once again, we squeezed through the opening in the grate. We climbed down and carefully made our way into the large round culvert.

To our surprise we found we could stand almost upright. This would make the walk easier. There was a trace of water in the large place, but plenty of light as we began our slow trek. We began to see spiders and bugs as we side stepped the shallow water. They seemed to enjoy being in this place like it was their home, well I suppose it was their home. So far, we had learned it was wet, buggy, creepy and scary in there.

As long as we had some light from the opening, things were all right. As we continued it became increasingly dim. George had the flashlight as he walked just ahead of me, but he waited too long to turn it on in my opinion. I found great comfort when there was that glowing beam of light.

As we came nearer to what must have been just beneath the center of the ball field, there was not just dampness and darkness, but strange noises. George acted brave, but he did appreciate having that flashlight right then.

"George, do you hear that, it sounded like dripping and what is that skittering sound?" There were strange squeaking noises following the scurrying sounds. This could not be a good thing, what in the heck were we doing in here?

"Oh gee, do we really want to see those things right now?" George spoke quietly with a tremor in his voice. He kept the beam of light aimed straight ahead, not down into the watery home of who knows what. We were both thinking the same thing, did we really want to see what we were hearing?

We did let the light help guide us, but we just wanted to get to the other side and quickly. Neither one of us looked down and tried to walk with our feet as high up on the pipe as we could.

"Keep out of the water, it has to be bad in the water," I whispered, as if that made any difference at this point. My voice reflected the depth of worry and fear I was feeling just at that moment in our pipe trek.

Funny how those two Bologna and cheese sandwiches we had so carefully wrapped in the wax paper, did not seem very inviting right now. My stomach was doing somersaults. George was way too quiet.

"George, are you all right? You are not saying anything." I was starting to panic. If something was wrong with George, what would I do? He was the one who liked all these creepy crawly things. I only liked them because he did.

"I'm here," he said a little too loudly. "Everything is fine. See there is light coming up ahead, just a little pale light," he added with a tense voice.

"Yeah, sure, pale light. It is pitch black in here if we didn't have that flashlight's glow." Talk about stating the obvious, but I was nervous, and my stomach was in such a knot that it might never be normal again.

Just then that flashlight began to flicker. George and I gasped at the same time. Being who he was, George gave that flashlight a thump against his palm to shake up the batteries. After another flicker it once again gave us a strong beam of light. Whew, that was scary. Neither one of us said a word, we just continued.

But then I found my louder voice, "There are more squeaks, and scurries, and creepies and crawlies, cobwebs, and water and I want out of here right now!" I had snapped a little at that point.

"And where in the heck is that hoped for pale light ahead?" I finished asking.

"There it is. I see light, we are coming to the end!" George said at last. This time he sounded happy and excited. I could tell the difference.

"Hey, something just ran over my foot, and it was furry and fast. I am out of here now," I yelled. So, we held hands and ran the final distance into the now dimming light of the woods.

Looking at each other, with our hearts racing from the adventure, we just started laughing. We had done something crazy, but we did it and we were glad.

We sat by that beautiful stream in the dimness of the woods surrounded by moss and ferns and ate the now rather squished sandwiches. We talked about what kind of bugs and creatures we saw. We also wondered about the ones we could only imagine. Yeah, it was a fun adventure all right.

Later we learned that this culvert was in fact a large storm drain that took the runoff rain and water away. Evidently there were times when the water would build up so rapidly, it ran through that drainpipe quite swiftly.

Oh Boy, were we glad we did not know that when we had our *Great McKoy Park Pipe Adventure*. We might have thought a little longer about our decision to travel through that drainpipe. Then again, we may have done the exact same thing. Yep, we would have done just that.

That big pipe lark in the park with George would surely be one of my favorite crazy things we did. Yes, it could have turned out differently I suppose, but right then none of that mattered.

I am glad we had our Great Adventure. I planned to enjoy my life's journey and every stop along the way.

CHAPTER SEVENTEEN

Big Wheels, Big Trouble

As you can imagine, automobiles were a huge part of our family. We had all learned to spot and name the model, make and year of each car on the road. In fact, naming these automobiles became a game or contest to pass the time on our road trips. Usually, we spotted Fords and Chevrolets for our games.

If we saw a car carrier rolling down the highway with the cars covered, we knew they were brand new models. Oh, we wanted a peek at those mysterious vehicles so badly. No one was allowed to see the new models until they were revealed with great majesty and grand presentations. This kept the mystique and thrill going for all the car lovers.

There was a true romance with people and cars. We talked about them, carefully leaned on them, polished them and showed them off to anyone who would show an interest in their prized possession.

My brothers Kenny and Tommy proudly drove the car slowly up and down the street so that everyone could admire their perfectly waxed, beautifully maintained automobile. Their pride and joy would be their own shiny cars.

When we moved from Waycross to Decatur, we drove our 1950 Ford Sedan. It was a showstopper because of the new paint color of chartreuse (yes that greenish-yellow color) and it was equipped with an official siren.

Daddy was still a law enforcement officer as a government agent, so he drove a government car. We were thrilled if he ever turned that siren on, which was rarely. But boy those times he did we grinned and felt so important riding in that screeching chartreuse Ford.

Our love affair with cars was strong and was first nurtured by our watchful Daddy as he studied and checked out each new car's statistics. The unveiling of the new models was akin to uncovering a shiny pot of gold. We saw a lot of his smiles when he was in his car-searching mode.

"Would you three like to go downtown to the Ford Dealership with me?" Daddy would ask ever so casually. The giveaway for Daddy's being very happy or very worried was that he rattled the coins in his pockets. The louder the rattle, the more urgency there was.

Tommy spoke up first. He was counting the days until he could drive a car by himself. Naturally thinking of having his own brand-new shiny car one day made him happy. Even though that would be a faraway time for him, he could dream.

"Sure, we'll go with you. Is Mama going too?" Tommy carefully asked.

That was a loaded question and the three of us studied Daddy's face for his response. He worked his mouth around just a bit and finally spoke.

"You know, I think she has a lot of laundry to do today. She most likely would rather stay home."

Rather stay home? You mean would she rather have a skunk loose in the house or go look at one more car? We knew better than to even broach the subject of new cars with our mother.

We did, however, feel as though we were sneaking out of the house that Saturday morning. No, that was probably our imagination. Surely Daddy had asked her to go with us. On the other hand, he did like things peaceful and free of drama. We drew our own conclusions.

All of us shared Daddy's infatuation with seeing a new car for the very first time. No other aroma could match opening the door of a brand-new car and inhaling that fragrance. Just looking at the dashboard with its new dials, and gauges caused our hearts to skip a beat. Nor was anything as brilliant as the gleaming paint and chrome on each shiny new model. Look at those fins and that grill and those white walls, man oh man!

Yet the biggest thrill was when you first entered the car showroom to see all the new and various models lined up in a gleaming row. Proud peacocks on display for everyone to adore; and we did. The whole new car experience was almost an overload for our senses. We could look, smell, hear, talk about but not touch. However, a salesman would allow us to have a close look if there was an interest in purchasing one of those brand-new automobiles.

That was never a problem because Daddy was always ready to buy one. He had to control that urge many times because he knew Mama would want to be informed of any impending large purchase. So, we just looked and enjoyed. We ooohed, and aaahed, and dreamed and had a grand time.

Another bonus was that any time we could be on an outing with our father when he was this relaxed and smiling, was a big deal for us. We all agreed that going to the showrooms was a unique adventure.

Our sister Patsy and brother Roy also enjoyed the lure of automobiles. Roy had always liked anything he could remake into something great, so he preferred the older used cars. Those were surely more readily available for him to transform into special vehicles. He possessed a keen mechanical mind that was full of ideas, always ready to transform something into a masterpiece.

Roy was now married, had a child and had to think of his own family and what was best for them. We all sat back in wonder watching him turn what would seem to us an insurmountable project into something magnificent. With his mind and talents, he could make those probabilities become his own possibilities. Their family would do just fine.

Patsy also was now a working adult who was learning the value of a dollar. She did not want to own a car herself, nor did she find it a necessary expense at that time of her life. She rode the trolley to work and usually carried her lunch. Patsy was really a good saver, thrifty with her wages and generous to our family.

It was that particular year of 1953 that she really wanted to make one of Daddy's dreams come true. Patsy and Daddy always had a special relationship. With that bond she could sense when Daddy was happy, upset, ready to tell a tale, or feeling excitement over some prospective project. She had sensed his feeling of wanting a car that was his personally, not a government work vehicle.

She understood and wanted to help. She had inherited her generous nature from our father. He would give, loan, or help any friend or family member who might need help at any time. We had all seen his many acts of helping others. Now Patsy wanted to help. She really wanted Daddy to have a new car that year.

This time Daddy took Patsy's generosity to help them purchase the new family car. She and he shopped together and chose a sleek green and white 1953 Chevrolet Sedan. What a beauty with its adornment of bright chrome and wide white-wall tires. It was sporty and sleek! Also, since they purchased the model at the end of the year, they were able to buy it for a good price.

As beautiful and elegant as this car was, it did not stay on our list of favorites. Let me give you the whole story about this doomed car.

At the end of December 1953, Mother took a special trip by airplane to Sudbury, Massachusetts. This was where Roy and Margie now lived, and they were about to bring their second child into the world.

Stevie, who was born January of 1952, was not quite two years old at this point, so Mama was happy to help out, as she always was. Their second son, Robert Carl Reach was born December 30, 1953. Bobby was a second grandchild and made both Mother and Daddy proud to see Roy's family growing.

The day Mama was due to return from her trip, was a chilly January day. Our family all went to the Atlanta Municipal Airport to pick up our mother on her return home. It was car trip filled with excitement and anticipation.

You see we knew we were about to give her a big surprise, one that had been well planned.

After hugging Mama, we started our walk to the car. As we made our way down the lines of cars in the parking lot, a cold misty rain began to fall and then it came down harder and colder.

Daddy gave us a wink and said, "Libby, let's just get into this car here and wait out the rain."

Well, Mama was mortified, "Roy Reach, for Heaven's Sake, we cannot do that! Someone might come and see us in this brand-new car and arrest us."

Things were not going as planned. After several awkward moments of pure unseen tension, Daddy finally admitted that this was, in fact, our very own new car.

That proud announcement was not well received. After giving him an icy stare, Mama proceeded to have a conniption fit otherwise known as *Lizzy's Tizzy*.

She began her tirade with these words, "Do you mean you purchased this without talking with me? Here we are with all of us working so hard and all the bills we have…" and so it went.

The silence as we rode home in that beautiful sedan was almost scary quiet. Our brand new 1953 Chevy had already lost its luster.

Thankfully, Daddy traded that car in for a 1955 powder blue, four-door Buick, a thing of beauty and a joy to behold! Mother did not seem to mind this purchase quite so much. He managed to do well in the trade in, plus this Buick was an especially grand automobile. She did like looking grand it seemed.

That beautiful blue Buick became my personal sanctuary. I would sometimes just sit in the car and daydream. Other times I would listen to the radio and read a book. I knew just how long I could play the radio so as not to run the battery down. Some lessons were learned the hard way.

Just when we thought everything had settled down for a couple of years, Daddy got the new car itch once more. I am not sure what caused his desire to trade in that magnificent powder blue Buick. However, when we saw the car that he proudly drove into the driveway in that year of 1957, we understood.

Up came the biggest car we had ever owned and possibly one of the biggest cars we had ever seen. By then I was almost fourteen years old, and my eyes grew huge just thinking of trying to drive that mammoth automobile.

It was a pale green, not chartreuse, 1957 Buick, the exceptionally large Road Master. It was so very long that the back of the car did not make it all the way into the carport. We might have to move just to house all these cars.

The pale green mammoth mobile managed to live long at the Reach house.

CHAPTER EIGHTEEN

Smaller Wheels, Still Trouble

"Hey, how about going for a Bike ride with me?" My friend Sarah, who we now called Shay, asked one Saturday Summer morning.

Man alive, her timing was perfect! I thought with relief.

Just prior to Shay's arrival I had been complaining to Mama, "There is nothing to do around here; I'm bored."

I knew from many past experiences that voicing such a complaint might end in a very unsatisfactory manner. Saying that was not a smart thing to do.

As expected, my mother immediately chirped out her suggestions, "Well, my goodness, Judy, there are certainly a lot of things I can think of to keep you busy."

I rolled my eyes and rued the moment I had said anything.

"I have some ironing you can do, some beans you can snap, some corn you can shuck, or some dusting to do in the Living Room." Oh boy, she just loved this conversation and all her great suggestions for keeping me entertained.

"Which of those fun things would you like to do?" she inquired while trying to keep a serious look on her face.

"That's OK, Mama, I think I hear somebody coming up the driveway," I quickly blurted.

Somebody please come up the driveway, I thought.

This was not going to be a car ride this time. Shay and I were going to ride our smaller than a car two-wheeled transportation. My beautiful red bicycle was my proudest possession and had become a monumental part of my life. Sarah felt the same about her blue and white bicycle. These bikes meant freedom and independence, and fun.

Mama almost laughed, but she just smiled as she said, "Yes you may go for a ride, but remember to watch out for cars and don't go too far from our neighborhood."

"Sure, I am always careful." And I bolted.

Shay smiled as I came running out and we pedaled our wheels as fast as possible down Adams Street. As we turned onto Pharr Road, we saw Larry Abbey and he joined our ride. We worked our way over to the East Lake Country Club, stopping to watch the golfers and fancy cars. The clubhouse looked like an elegant mansion in Europe, just like the ones I read about in books.

Leaning on the handlebars, I dreamed of the day I would ride up in a fancy new car then be escorted into that elaborate clubhouse. We would have a fine and fancy candlelight dinner served by waiters with silver trays. Naturally I would be on the arm of a nice fellow for this special date. It would happen; I would make it happen one day.

That day we rode all the way to Candler, heading toward Glenwood. It was a little too far for us to go with the traffic getting heavier, so the three of us decided to turn around. Usually, like that day, we ended up back at McKoy Park where we could all go our separate ways without being too far from home. That day we had taken one more detour to East Lake Center.

Suddenly there was my older brother on his bike, standing right in our way. I braked to a halt at the sight of Tommy as he straddled his bike with his arms folded trying to look very stern. He could not carry off stern at all.

"Why are you at the park?" I asked innocently.

"Aw, Mama made me come and find you. You all have been gone a long time you know." He looked more irritated than mad at me.

"Well, we're OK and all is safe and sound, see?"

"Yeah, and I see you went to East Lake for ice cream at Wilson's."

Tommy pointed to my pedal pushers. Strawberry stains were running down those white pedal pushers. Oops!

"So, what, you go all over the place and stay gone half the day," I pouted. This was not a valid argument. Then I added, "Anyway we stopped at Susan Huff's house for a little while."

"Don't you think I can go twice as far on my bike since I am four years older than you? You're still a little kid, you know." He had to gloat, didn't he?

Smugness, I hated smugness and I hated being treated like a little child. So, this exchange would surely end with my poking out my bottom lip, then riding home after giving a small wave to my fellow adventurers.

Shay and Larry smiled. They weren't laughing, were they? They better not have been laughing. It was bad enough to be retrieved like a lost dog by my brother.

Tommy quickly pulled ahead of me and took off like Mr. Lightening Wheels just to show off. He was quite happy with himself. I was not impressed.

That was just one more fun summer day spent on my own two wheels, with my friends.

I must tell you though that many of the even smaller wheels had a place in my heart. They gave me hours of enjoyment from the time I had memory in Waycross. On those dirt roads, before Clifton Grove was paved, we would pull or be pulled by our Red Flyer Wagon.

Being the youngest and smallest it was easy to figure out who was being pulled by my brother. When I was the puller the red flyer wagon might be filled with my dolls, marbles, smooth chunks of glass for playing a game of hopscotch and my little bag of ball and jacks.

If Mama didn't see me run out the door, I managed to grab a cookie or cracker. I ran out and ran away a lot, but only to the close neighbors. If no one was around there was no problem playing with this assortment of games all by myself.

Sometimes I would push myself along with my wooden scooter, but I had to be on a paved road because the wheels got all clogged up in the dirt. I could always just bounce a ball. This was all part of my fun and games. Now that I was older, I could go much further and much faster.

In Decatur there was no shortage of friends to accompany me. I no longer felt the need to run away as I had done in Waycross. Naturally being older I was much wiser at ten instead of four and felt more responsible for my actions.

That's what my brothers kept trying to make me understand anyway. Having a younger sister shadowing their every move made Kenny and Tommy reach this conclusion. Brothers sometimes had strange ideas.

Much smaller wheels than bikes or wagons were next in line for some fun activity. These would be my shiny metal roller skates that clamped onto my shoes, my very sturdy-soled shoes. I also had to wear a skate key on a string around my neck to tighten each skate clamp if it got loosened. There was a smoothly paved skating oval just beyond our back yard near the McKoy pool so we could skate anytime we desired.

Sometimes four or five of us would link hands to go faster around the turns. Even though those skates were heavy and clunky, we managed to gain speed to whip around those tight turns. We also managed to do fancy steps, spins, and jumps. There were skinned knees and lots of bruises, but we always went back for more. Sometimes if a cut was bleeding, it would mean a quick run home for a Band-Aid, then back for more fun.

The most daring skating act was when we attempted to skate down Lenore Street off South Adams, near to our house. This was a long sloping road leading to the busy McDonough Street. Here again we suffered many scraped knees and elbows while trying to execute that hill and yet we would get up and go again.

If we saw the end of the street coming near and could not stop in time, we had to veer into the curb and usually fall headlong into someone's yard. Yes, that was great fun! What were a few bruises when you feel the air running through your hair and your heart racing fast because of the danger of skating down that hill?

Then there were the scooters that we stood on with one foot, pushing with the other foot to gain speed while holding on to the raised handle. This could be a very unsatisfactory mode of transport, but it did go downhill nicely; going back up was always a chore.

Now times were changing, and I was growing more independent so naturally the best choice of wheels had to be those on bicycles. We had two choices for bikes, a boy's, or a girl's bike. It made it easy to decide which kind to ride. Most bicycles had big tires that made the rides smoother.

Many bikes looked alike except for having or not having a middle bar; we just wanted a neat color. Red was my choice and did I love my bicycle! To make my own set of wheels even more special, I would clip cards onto the spokes of the tires to create a cool sound the faster I pedaled.

There was a ledge on the back to carry a friend, and sometimes even carry someone on the handlebar but avoiding Lenore Street if riding this loaded down. Tassels hanging from the handlebars and if needed, a basket on the front would complete my perfect vehicle. Oh yeah buddy, I was cool!

We rode around the park and nearby streets at first, but it didn't take long to venture much further into other neighborhoods. The world was at our feet; if we could keep pedaling, we could keep riding. We knew how to put the chains back on if they fell off. Also, a trip to the gas station for a fill up of air in our tires might be needed. Of course, at home we had a hand pump and oil can.

Our scope of rides gradually increased until we would be miles away from home, but most of the time we rode to the East Lake shopping center. We did not worry or think about any dangers, we just had fun and enjoyed our bike rides

Somebody surely watched over children on smaller wheels.

Judy and Carole doing Dress Up Day Carol, Judy, Laura, Marcia, neighbor friends

Fifth Avenue 5th Grade Class, Mrs. Patterson

1st Row: David Mobley, Billy Rhodes, Freddy Nicholson, Larry Abbey, Neal Pharr, Charles Jordon

2nd Row: Butch Luther, Linda Moss, Bobby Mauney, Sarah Kneale, Joyce and Janyce McClung, Joy Oxford, Tommy Goddard, Becky Clapp, Ronald Evans

3rd Row: Donald Armistead, Chip Conyers, Dorinda Wadleton, Judith Broderick, George Bass, George Mitchell, Carolyn Watson, Blake McLeod, Kenneth Nation, John White

4th Row: Mrs. Patterson, Marion Brewton, Gail Brand, Tim Jackson, Christine Chewing, Billy Bridges, David Robinson, Judy Reach, Betty Lide, Susan Huff

Games and Toys of the '50s

Board Games

Chutes n Ladders • Parcheesi • Monopoly • Dominoes • Bingo Scrabble Clue • Operation • Chinese checkers • Cribbage • Candy Land • Checkers Chess • Card games such as Canasta • Bridge • Poker • Old Maid Concentration • Solitaire

Toys

Spinning Tops • Doll house • Lincoln Logs • Erector Sets • Toy Trains Wood Blocks • Mr. and Mrs. Potato Heads • Tiddly Winks • Etch a sketch • Paper Dolls • Silly Putty • Slinky • Cootie • Magic Ball • Toy Rifle • Cowboy outfits and plastic figures • View Master • Kaleidoscope • Miniature farm sets and plastic figures • Barbie Doll • Baby Dolls • Toy Drum • Matchbox Cars • Pop Guns • BB Guns

Outside Games

Ball 'n Jacks • Hopscotch • Jump Rope • Hula Hoop • Kick the Can Red Rover Red Rover • King of the Mountain • Leap Frog • Sling the Statue • Hide and Seek • Pick up Sticks • Roller skates • Hopscotch Bicycles • Push Scooters • Stick and Street ball • Wagons • Marbles Pogo Sticks • Croquet • Badminton • Red Light Green Light

Pastimes and Activities

Movies • Picnics • Swimming • Football • Basketball • Tennis • Ping Pong Baseball • Softball • Taking Rides in Cars • Eating Out at Restaurants Long Walks • Symphony Concerts • Musical Concerts • Museums Dancing Circus • Fairs

Best of all having groups of friends with whom you could play street games, talk, walk, gossip and laugh.

Chapter Nineteen

Storm Clouds

"Roy, Roy!" My Mother was half sobbing as she called Daddy's name.

"Can you hear me? Please open your eyes. Let me hear you breathe!"

One by one each of us slowly entered the Living Room where Mama was Kneeling on the floor next to the chair where Daddy was sitting. He was not sitting straight; something was not right. Kenny, Tommy, and I were struck with silence as we watched and heard Mother's tearful words.

She laid her head close to his chest to hear his breathing.

"Oh, Praise the Lord," she said in a relieved voice, "He has a shallow breath." She seemed to say this into the air as if not saying it to any person. It was almost like a prayer of thanks to God. She had a strong faith. The three of us felt her faith at that moment, right then.

"Tommy, call the Emergency Number for an ambulance," she said at last in a low determined voice. He didn't move, none of us moved.

"Now, Tommy, quickly, your Daddy is having a heart attack," she said in a louder voice.

Hearing these words, Tommy quickly sprang into action and made the call. We had all heard these words once before when we lived in Waycross. Daddy had his first heart attack when he was just forty-six years old. That was a traumatic time in the Reach Family. A time of fear and dread not knowing what was going to happen to our Daddy.

He was in the hospital and none of us could see him except for Mother and Patsy. Roy, Jr. had already moved to Atlanta with Margie at that point to attend Georgia Tech. Once again Patsy became the helper and comforter to our mother and the caretaker for us children.

Patsy adored Daddy; everyone knew that. They had so much in common, even their mannerisms and humor were alike. Though she knew what she had to do, it had been a terribly emotional time for her. Mother had been beside herself during that first heart attack in Waycross.

Now here was Mother once again having to watch her Roy go through this pain and watch him be near death and experiencing it all over again. This day happened to be Easter Sunday. We had all been dressed in our new clothes after attending church. Easter was very important to the Reach family with our faith-filled upbringing.

Mother had made me a new dress, bought me a new hat with ribbons and even bought me little strappy white shoes with lace topped socks. The boys had their jackets and ties on and dress trousers, looking nice. We had been having a wonderful day.

We had come home ready for the ham dinner Mother had prepared and kept in the oven. She had made sweet potatoes, snapped beans and rolls. Oh yes, and a yellow cake with fluffy white frosting topped with jellybeans and gumdrops. I had helped decorate that beautiful cake.

Patsy had helped us boil the eggs on Saturday. After we wrote our names on our eggs with crayons, we carefully balanced them on the little wires to lower them into the cups of vinegar and dye. Next, we put the pink, blue, green and yellow eggs into baskets with the green grassy stuff. I had just loved doing all that with the family.

But all that was yesterday. This was today, the day that everything was different. Then a lot began to happen in the next few hours. We were all upset about Daddy, but I did not know exactly what was happening or what to do.

Patsy would help us when she got back from going to the Methodist Church with her new boyfriend. I knew she was going to be upset, but we needed her. I always needed her.

The ambulance screaming down Spring Street was frightening to hear. There was a big hullaballoo when those men hurried in to get Daddy onto a stretcher. Tommy, Kenny and I stood in the Dining Room out of the way while this was going on in front of us. It was frightening.

Mother followed them out the door and down the stairs to the driveway and got into the ambulance with Daddy. Now what were we supposed to do? Yes, Mother knew.

"Kenny, come here please," she spoke in a tone I had never heard.

Kenny knew how to hustle, and he did. "Yes, Ma'am, what do I do?"

"This is important. Now listen to me, you get Tommy and Judy into our car and drive to the Emory University Hospital. Do you remember how to get there?" she said urgently.

"Yes ma'am, I drove to the hospital last time when Daddy saw his doctor. Remember?"

"Good, now be careful, drive safely and take care of your brother and sister. Can you do that for me?" she pleaded. There was no misunderstanding what she meant to happen.

"Sure, sure Mama, I can do that." Kenny also spoke in a low voice. "I will watch out for them. I guess I am the only one old enough to go into the hospital so I will find out where they take Daddy."

Then he added in a worried voice, "Okay, Mama, is that what I should do?"

Kenny spoke these words in such a low and slow tone I could barely hear him. But I heard Mama say that was good. Then they were gone, sirens blaring again. It was all so very frightening. I think this day will be in my memory for a long time. Things seemed to change in those moments in the Reach household that day.

Mama had known Patsy would be there soon to help us get through this frightening time. That Easter Sunday when I was 10, Tommy and Kenny were 14 and 16, we all seemed older just then as we watched that white ambulance carry our parents to Emory Hospital.

We did not know what would happen next. I was frightened and crying. Tommy was very quiet. But Kenny began dashing around to find the keys to the Chevrolet and ordered us to get in the car. Good Golly, he did get us there safe and sound even though he was obviously frightened.

Tommy and I stayed with the car as we waited. After a while the time was passing slowly, and we were restless. He was not sure how to act in this unusual situation. Then he took the basket of Easter eggs and said he would hide them for me to find. I wasn't sure if we should, but he went ahead to hide some of the eggs by the pretty creek next to where we were parked. Tommy was worried but was still sweet to me.

After his hiding and my finding the colorful hidden eggs, we both stood by that little creek looking down at the rippling water. It calmed us. I took his hand and smiled up at him. Tommy waited a few seconds before letting my hand go, a rare moment for me.

Daddy stayed in the hospital for over two weeks and during that entire time our house took on a different air, a quieter one. Patsy cooked for us and took care of things while Mother was with Daddy in the hospital.

She kept us reassured even though we knew how worried she really was. When Daddy finally came home, we were expected to act quietly and calmly. How could that ever happen in the Reach Household?

We did whatever we were told. When Daddy had that heart attack, we all knew just what we had to do. Whatever it would take to get our Daddy strong and healthy once again was exactly what we were all prepared to do. He was Daddy. We needed him.

The day Mama called me into the room to see Daddy in the bed I was a little fearful. He looked paler than his usual tanned face and he was not smiling as big as usual. I walked slowly over and said, "Daddy, I missed you." I did not know what to say and I was hoping to not cry. Then he gave me one of his Daddy smiles and patted my hand. I felt relieved and happy.

"We are going to try to be quiet so you can rest, OK?" I croaked.

"I am sure you will, Judy." He said my name. Then he smiled sweetly. I smiled and left.

Our Daddy was our Daddy again and he was home, and our family was together. It was good.

CHAPTER TWENTY

To Curse or Not to Curse

"Kenny, are you going to drive to East Lake Center?" I asked my brother warily, but with anticipation.

"Yeah, why do you want to know?"

"Well, I was thinking you might let me go with you," I continued hopefully.

"I don't know about that because later Tommy and I might want to take a ride around Decatur," Kenny replied in a lack-luster manner.

Then I quickly suggested, "Let me just go to the drug store with you two and then you can bring me back home." Thinking quickly, I added, "Anyway, Daddy needs you to get some tobacco for his pipe and you have to bring that back to him, right?"

Kenny stared down at me with a look of disgusted resignation; he knew I would keep whining at him until he finally would give in to my plea.

"Alright, I guess you can ride along, just this time." Then he added, "Go get Tommy and hurry up so we can get going."

Kenny tossed this comment to me over his shoulder as he went out of the kitchen door, letting the screen slam shut behind him, naturally. He was already grabbing the keys out of his blue jeans pocket and running his fingers quickly through his wavy blond hair as he headed to the Blue Goose, his navy-colored Dodge sedan that was parked in the driveway.

Tommy bolted out of the house also letting the door slam. I quickly told him, "Kenny said I can go with y'all for a little while."

He gave me a quick wink, bent down to make sure the cuffs on his jeans were folded perfectly, then caught a quick glance at his reflection in the window. He gently patted his brown flat top, freshly groomed with Butch wax, making sure each hair was standing tall.

As he passed me, I got a slight whiff of Daddy's Old Spice and thought to myself, "This can't be good; both are trying to look all spiffy. That means they are going to make sure they ditch me right away so they can cruise around town."

Oh well, I would take what I could get. Any ride with my big brothers in Kenny's cool car was a thrill for me. It made me feel important and proud to have them as brothers.

As I sat in the middle of the back seat, I leaned forward with my arms propped on the back of the front seat and my head stuck in between Kenny and Tommy. Now I could see everything and everywhere.

I had to take advantage of this rare time with both my brothers in the car, with only me, not a bunch of their friends crammed into the back seat. This was a treat.

When we pulled up to the East Lake Drug Store, Kenny handed me a dollar bill and told me to run into the pharmacy for the tobacco.

Then he leaned out the car window and called after me, "Don't forget to put the change in the bag for Daddy."

After carefully selecting just the right pouch of fragrant, loose briar tobacco, I made my way to the cash register. I handed my purchase to the lady behind the counter and asked her to please put the change in the same bag.

She was a tall stern-looking lady wearing large glasses and her hair was pulled back in a tight bun.

Hair done up in buns and big glasses make a scary combination, I thought to myself.

She glared at me over her lowered glasses and slowly asked, "Young lady, just who is this tobacco for anyway?"

With a feeling of panic setting in and knowing that my face was turning red, I managed to blurt out, "It's for my Daddy and he said it was alright for me to buy it for him."

She reluctantly handed me the bag with a slight *tsk, tsk*.

I took that paper sack and ran across the shiny white-and-black-tiled floor so fast I almost slipped down. I jumped breathlessly into the backseat and slammed the door securely behind me.

Then I innocently sputtered, "Boy, what a Witch that lady was!"

Well, *witch* was the word I thought I said. Evidently the word that did come out of my mouth started with a *B*. Tommy and Kenny both spun their heads around and almost climbed over the back of the front seat as they yelled at me in unison, "Hey, don't you ever use that kind of language!"

"What do you mean? I hear you say that word and lots of others all the time," I quickly sputtered.

They looked at each other, again saying the same thing at the same time, "That's different, we are guys."

Out went my lower lip as I crossed my arms. This was the usual position I assumed when going into a pout mode.

My brothers would usually roll their eyes and say, "Look out, Judy the Cootie's got her lip poked out so far she might trip on it."

Boy, that was just too funny, wasn't it? I thought.

After what seemed like a forever-long silence, my brother Tommy turned back to me and said softly, "Well, one of us probably should have gone in to buy Daddy's pouch of tobacco instead of you."

Always the gentle peacemaker my brother Tommy was. Perhaps I would, or could, or should take a few directions from them about what I should and should not say. After all I did want to be a nice girl.

Speaking of directions, this began my many lessons in proper lady-like behavior from my wise older siblings.

"Judy don't sit that way. Keep your skirt pulled down over your knees. Cross your legs like a lady." "Don't say crude words. Never act stuck up."

"Speak to people only in the way you would like to be spoken to yourself."

And so it went until I thought I would never learn how to be a perfect young lady. The good thing was having the attention of both my brothers. Yeah, that was kind of a cool thing, so I listened.

Now there was one thing our mother would not abide, and that was cursing. If she ever heard any one of us take the Lord's name in vain, her soft brown hair with its loose waves would stand on end. Her gentle Hazel eyes would blaze. If she ever combined that fearsome look with her hands tightly held on her hips, watch out.

Now she did understand that Daddy's job entailed being around a lot of rough people. He had to chase down rascals who made and sold illegal whisky. He never knew what type of character he could encounter, tough, scary, mean or all the above plus using crude cuss words.

However, when he stepped through the door of our home, he was expected to resume his gentle and genteel ways. Our Daddy knew Mama, so he always did just that.

My sister Patsy had always been and always would be a lady and used correct language and proper manners. Of course, there may have been times when she was with her friends that she might be less than perfect, but never around Mama.

My brothers, on the other hand, liked to push the language barrier to the limit when it came to using expletives. Anything said with flair made more of an impact than using namby-pamby words. So, they did just that. Take the words Durn, or Durnit, I was only allowed to say darn!

Kenny and Tommy took a lot of heat for any colorful language. There was always a lot of heat.

For instance, the word of choice seemed to be Gosh, but that was the civilized pronunciation. More than likely, you would hear such variations as Gah, Gyah, or G-a-a-a. If they ever combined any form of Gosh with Dang or Durn to create the oath Gah-Dang, that is the point they would have gone over the top and entered the evil cussing zone.

When tempers flared in the heat of an argument, or even when a little sister would break a model airplane, it was best to cover your ears and exit the room.

After some worker hit his thumb with a hammer, you might hear, "Dang it almighty to hell and back, that hurt." Understandable expletives at such a time.

Naturally, I would never use any foul language because I did not like the repercussions. Like the word *witch* was no longer in my vocabulary; my said-out-loud vocabulary that is. I did seem to say Golly or Gee Whiz even Goodness Gracious or Gosh Darn It quite a bit, and those words barely slipped under the cursing radar.

Mama on the other hand, might be heard to utter some interesting words at times. "Lordy, would you look at the size of that laundry pile?" she could be heard to say. Or if she was frustrated beyond belief we might hear, "Lord Have Mercy on my Soul." We stepped back when we heard that.

"Oh, for Pity's Sake, what did you do now?" was another one we did not want to hear. We all looked around to see who she was talking about and hoped it was not one of us that time.

The most feared expletive would come from our usually mild-mannered Daddy. "Good Gosh All Mighty, what happened now?" Trouble ensued. Those words were never good for us to hear.

There were so many expletives, curse words, slang expressions and slurs that they would fill many books. Meanwhile new ones would crop up immediately.

Yes, there was a very fine line a young girl walked to maintain the standard of being a *Nice Girl.* I learned to carefully walk that line with the constant help given to me by my family.

Sometimes there seemed to be too many directions coming from too many different directions for me to comprehend.

Kenny and his 1950 Ford with glass-pack Mufflers, Tommy with Bill Scott by our 1957 Buick Roadster, the East Lake Pharmacy.

Slang and Cursing in the '50s

Knuckle Sandwich • Groovy • Gadzooks • Groovin' • No Sweat • Party Pooper • Make Like a Tree and Leave • Back Seat Bingo • Necking Spooning • Lock Lips • Made in the Shade • Yikes • Cool • Cool Cat Cool Dude • Cool Daddy • Eat Dirt • Hipster • Cootie • Burn Rubber Stuff It • Shut Your Trap • Put a Lid on It • Take a Chill Pill • Scram Get Lost • Shove Off • Get Outta' Here • Scat • Shoo • Get Bent • Chill Take a Chill Pill • Daddy-O • Ankle Biter • Shake It Up • Main Squeeze • Dating Seeing Someone • Going Out • Hanging • Shake It Up • What's Groovin' What's Shaking • Is that a Hickie on your neck?

Swear Words and Cursing

Dammit • Durn It • Dang • Oh Darn • For heaven's sake • Good Golly Miss Molly • Good Lord • Lord Almighty • Lord Have Mercy on My Soul • Oh Sugar • Shoot • Jiminy Cricket • Hells bells • Frickin' • Flippin' Jumping Jehosofat • Crud • Crap • Gee Whiz • Stuff it • Good Golly • Goodness Gracious • Good Gracious Sakes Alive • Golly • Gee Whiz • Geeze Oh Pete Bull Hockey • Holy Cow • Holy Crap • Oh Fudge • Oh Flip • Dag Blast It DagNabbit • Oh shoot • Gosh darn it

My own phrases

Cheese n' Crackers • Excuse me for Living • Holy Moley • Darn It

And never again did I call Anyone a Bitch or even a Witch!

Not included here are Foul words or any taking the name of the Lord in Vain, No No's!

CHAPTER TWENTY-ONE

Once Upon a Time Wedding

My sister had lots of friends from Waycross and from Mercer College, guys and girls. She had always made friends easily wherever she was. There were several fellows she considered as boyfriends, but really, they were all good friends.

Since Patsy had been living with us again and working at Rich's, her life was changing. In fact, there was someone new who seemed to come around the most and caused her eyes to shine the brightest. You see, she had recently been introduced to someone on a blind date. Our neighbor across the street, Mrs. Allie Kimbrell, worked at the Cotton Producers Association where she met a nice guy whom she wanted Patsy to meet.

Then I began thinking that now this will make four or five boyfriends she will have. *Goodness Gracious,* I was only ten and had a long way to go to have that many boyfriends. I had only one, George. The date was not that blind because she had a twinkle in her eye when he came around.

Tommy Cullens had recently graduated from the University of Georgia, and Mrs. Kimbrell thought he was a nice young man for Patsy. He was from a town in South Georgia, Camilla I think, not sure where that was. I would find out more about all this.

Their first date must have gone all right because they surely seemed to have their eyes on each other every time he came around to see her at our house. He was sort of cute and funny and seemed to like us kids because he would bring us ice cream and gifts. Tommy acted like he really enjoyed our whole family.

It became a bit confusing to have two Tommy's around the house, so Tommy Cullens started calling my brother a new name. Instead of William Thomas Reach, he called him *Willy-T*.

By the time I turned eleven their romance had blossomed so much that they decided to get married. *Married*, no, no, no, that would mean Patsy would go away and I probably would never ever see her again and then what would I do? What were they thinking?

Then she asked me to be a bridesmaid, well a Junior Bridesmaid in their wedding and things got a little better. I met and started being friends with Tommy's sister Louise's daughter, Beverly Booth and she was the other junior bridesmaid, how fun. Patsy and Tommy had lots of friends and family and this wedding was getting larger at every turn.

Tommy's Mother, Mrs. Sadie, was well known in Camilla for collecting beautiful antiques. She was a longtime member of the Garden Club and was a skilled flower arranger and gardener. Mr. Cullens also was a big notable in Camilla as he had a cotton gin company, ran the local newspaper, and even had been the mayor at one time. Wait a minute, this was getting to be a big deal for everyone.

There were a bunch of decisions, planning and compromises whirling around everywhere and all the time. It made my head spin and my mind work too hard, so I decided to let all those adults take care of that and I would just be Judy. The word *Wedding* became more than a word, it was an ever-consuming state.

Mother wanted them to be married in a First Baptist Church, but the Cullens were and always had been Methodists. So, they compromised and chose the beautiful big First Baptist Church in North Decatur and had the very prominent Dr. Charles L. Allen of Grace Methodist Church perform the wedding ceremony. Not only was he well known, his church on Ponce De Leon was the largest Methodist church in Georgia at that time. Patsy and Tommy had been alternating attending this Methodist church and the Baptist church. Well, there was one compromise successfully made.

Then came the subject of flowers for the wedding. As was noted, Mrs. Sadie Cullens knew her flowers; she had been arranging them with her Garden Club in Camilla for years, so it was only natural that she handled all that. Mother, wanting to use own her talent, sewed Beverly and my beautiful waltz length junior-bridesmaids gowns out of sea foam green voile. She also deftly sewed her own delicate blue lace dress adorned with rhinestones.

Their wedding had bridesmaids of Patsy's friends and Tommy's sisters, with groomsmen and ushers and probably many others that I could not know. I did know it was a big Fairy Tale Wedding with Patsy being the Princess and Tommy being the Prince.

Patsy, my lovely, petite sister was delicately adorned that day in her long white flowing wedding gown of satin, lace, and pearls. Tommy and Kenny were handsome in their suits and then Mother and Daddy looked wonderful in their fine outfits. Wouldn't you know; they too beamed with pride and joy along with Mr. and Mrs. Cullens. Everyone looked quite grand with smiles on their faces and perhaps a few tears of joy here and there, even in my eyes.

The reception was also perfect, being held at the church with lots of food and a gorgeous cake. It was a successful blending of planning, talent, and love. The most important reality was that on April 30, 1955, Mr. and Mrs. Tommy Cullens had a most splendid wedding to start their life together.

Indeed, it was a fantastic Fairy Tale Wedding.

After their honeymoon, Patsy and Tommy decided to buy a house in Tony Valley, which was not far from Spring Street. Maybe this new situation was going to work out after all. I mean Tommy did continue to bring us cool stuff and he was a lot of fun; plus, Patsy was happy.

Tommy did love to cut up and play jokes on people. Because we all knew this, he got the credit for pulling a fast one on Daddy; one that perhaps he had not done.

We had all gone to the big Home Show in Atlanta, spending the whole day looking at all the great new gadgets such as 18-inch TV screens in fancy console cabinets, ice boxes or that had their own door for the freezer part, and radios that were small enough to carry in your hand, neat stuff. Everyone dropped their names into as many raffle boxes as possible, had fun, and returned home before suppertime.

That same evening, we received a phone call, "May I please speak to Mr. Roy Reach?"

Well, it sure sounded like Tommy Cullens, so Daddy took the phone with a chuckle and heard, "Is this the Mr. Reach who lives on Spring Street?" the voice inquired.

Daddy went along with the joke and said, "Why, yes, it is." The voice continued, "Well, Mr. Reach I have good news for you, you have won our modern, state-of-the art RCA Hi-Fi Record player and radio in a lovely wood console."

Daddy laughed into the phone and said, "OK Tommy, that's enough, you can stop now. You know we never win anything."

"But Sir, if you will just come back to the Home Show…," the persistent voice continued, "We will be glad to help load your prize into your car."

Daddy laughed again and said, "Yep, we'll be right there." He immediately called Tommy to say to him, "You got me good this time."

"What do you mean, Sir?" Tommy asked in genuine surprise.

"That's enough; you know I didn't win any fancy Hi Fidelity machine," Daddy chuckled.

With a true surprise in his voice Tommy replied, "Sir, that wasn't me and to prove it I will ride down with you right now to the Home Show!"

Wouldn't you know, they did just that and to our astonishment they brought home the most beautiful Hi-Fi console we had ever seen. It was complete with a turntable for 78, 33 1/3, and 45 rpm records, Plus a radio.

All was right; we could tell by the way Daddy proudly beamed. That new addition to our home should bring years of entertainment and joy for our family.

The prank that never was a prank ended in a triumph!

CHAPTER TWENTY-TWO

Cultivating My Culture

"Hey, did you guys get the news yet? We have to go take dancing lessons and learn table manners in some class." John White announced this to the posse of boys outside the steps at Fifth Avenue.

Loud voices quickly rang out, "Whatcha' talking about? Naw, No Way; I am not goin', You gotta' be kidding, dancing, shoot no," and so forth. Some of them had picked up some pretty colorful language by then, so I will not go further into the actual remarks.

No, this news was not being received with favor as John had already known. He was relishing being the deliverer of this nauseating news to the guys.

"Who says we gotta' go to this dumb class anyway? I think you are making this up just to sound good in front of the girls," Donald yelled in his loud voice. Neal Pharr and Larry Abbey perked up at that remark, now what?

John was realizing he better deliver the second half of the news, "Well, you don't have to go, but they would really like you to attend, I guess. There is going to be some big dance at the end of the classes with punch and stuff," he snorted.

"Dance, you mean we have to dance with girls? Well, can we pick who we dance with 'cause maybe I can think of some girls I wouldn't mind dancing with too much," Larry chimed in with a little apprehension.

"Let's go in and find out the details before you guys get any more upset. Geeze, I am sorry John told you now, you buncha' idiots," Blakie McLeod said, laughing as he said that. He was likable and funny and could get away with such a remark.

George had not joined in with the disparaging remarks. In fact, he caught my eye but quickly looked away. We both knew it would be fun and a different adventure to try. It was nice having him as my boyfriend.

Meanwhile the girls were a gaggle of giggling geese hearing the news. "Dancing, with boys, prom dresses, corsages, boys, manners, and boys maybe being nice. This is going to be a dream. Let's all sign up for this class."

It was well received at home of course. Mother immediately started thinking ahead, "You already know your table manners, and you are a polite girl. If it will be dance and etiquette, you can learn something more I suppose."

Then she kept thinking, and asked, "Where is this class being held and who is teaching it?"

"It's at one of those big houses on Adams Street. Miss Rena Grizell, I think is her name. She has a room all set up for dancing and a big dining room to show us table manners."

"I believe the teacher said Etiquette, but the boys kept griping about what that was. They were told all that meant was good manners. I like the word Etiquette myself," I happily added.

Mother nodded and let me keep talking. She knew well that when I was excited about something I tended to ramble, so ramble on I did.

"A dance at the end means a new dress and I hope George is the one to take me. Oh, the girls are very excited. That is all we have been talking about. That is all the boys are talking about too. *Gripe, Gripe, Gripe* was all we heard."

When the boys' groaning and moaning, fussing, and cussing ended, a lot of them did sign up for the class. My friends George and Shay attended naturally, and many more classmates had joined. When those classes did take place there were quite a few girls and surprisingly, even some boys.

None of us knew what to expect after we arrived that first day. The girls saw only fun and joy ahead. Looking at the huddle of boys, I think they visualized being eaten alive by a big thing called Etiquette. Too bad for them.

As it turned out, all of us liked Miss Grizell; she was kind and elegant. They were such wonderful lessons that I soon was able to ballroom dance and know how to act more graceful and charming. At least it was something close to that; after all I was still a pre-teen. The boys endured the class, but we noticed some of them had small smiles. But if they caught another guy's eye, they had to moan and groan for appearance's sake.

There we were in her home after a few lessons, and the boys still squirmed and fidgeted while the girls smiled and eagerly waited to be asked to dance. Will they ever change? After we advanced from the basic box step to the waltz and more complicated dances, Miss Rena felt we were ready for our big dance. She said it would be held at an actual ballroom in town, a big ballroom.

It was all going to be too grand in that big ballroom. I did get a new dress that Mother made me. It was a lovely lilac tulle dress with a tea length full skirt and even a matching stole. George gave me a wrist corsage and his mother drove us to the Ball, and for a twelve-year-old, that was heaven.

Seeing the girls all dressed up in fancy dresses and the boys in jackets and ties, it looked almost like a dream to me. Somehow, the boys didn't look as enchanted as the girls. Wasn't that strange? They pulled on their ties, ran their fingers around their shirt collars as if they were being choked and generally looked uncomfortable. Some of them had their hair slicked down and parted in a way that only their mothers would have done. We had to hide our giggles.

"Isn't this the best night ever in the whole wide world?" I said to Shay. She smiled and nodded. She was even prettier than usual in her new pink lacy dress. George overheard me and looked up at the ceiling. There must have been something interesting on the ceiling because a lot of the boys seem fixated on it that night.

All the girls had on a little lipstick and rouge and naturally some of them filled out their dresses in a curvier manner than some of us. Dorinda, Judith, and Marian had been noticed already by the boys. Our day will come, we hoped.

After a great deal of feet shuffling the boys stayed seated in their chairs with their hands in their pockets. They looked so glum it was like someone told them there was no more ice cream on the planet.

I must admit us girls did not help as we seemed to congregate in groups of giggles and stares. Hey, we knew manners and etiquette now, we should be prepared for this grand night.

Miss Rena anticipated exactly such actions on our parts. She finally entered the room looking elegant in a pale green satin dress with matching heels. Oh my, being an adult sure made clothes fit a lot better than they did on a twelve-year old.

She silently gave the boys encouraging nods toward the girls and lifted her palm up with a reminder to stand tall. She caught our eyes and gave us the breakup the groups sign with her hands. We did, and they did finally ask each of us to dance. At first, we all stiffly did the box step in our fine clothes. My skirt was so full with the stiff crinolines, that it made George seem three feet from me.

I didn't mind any of that, I was dancing in a Ballroom with a beautiful new gown with my boyfriend and a corsage. We also had our pictures taken, oh yes, this must have been the best time ever. It was a magical night to remember for me and I hoped for everyone else, but I knew not everyone ever shared my enthusiasm at such times.

Not too long after learning all that etiquette, I was in for another cultural experience. One day my sister came to give the terrific news, that she had purchased a piano for the family. Oh my, what a surprise, a beautiful blond Kimball upright. It was very pretty and brand sparkling new.

When it was delivered, I saw that our mother was pleased as punch. We soon learned why; she was a skilled piano player. She had played the piano at many church functions and Sunday School in Waycross. She was doing the same here at Fifth Avenue First Baptist, now to be able to play one at home would be wonderful for her.

She knew a lot of songs that were not played in the church, like Ragtime and Boogie-Woogie Blues! What a grand command she had over those black and white keys. It was a thrill for us to listen and watch as her fingers flew across the ivories in up-tempo ragtime like *I'll be Down to Get You in a Taxi Honey*, *Toot, Toot, Tootsie, Goodbye*, or ballads like the *Tennessee Waltz*.

Sometimes as she played for us from the Baptist Hymnal, the family would gather around to sing in harmony to our favorite hymns like *The Old Rugged Cross*, *Whispering Hope*, *Onward Christian Soldiers*, or *How Great Thou Art*.

Mother gave me piano lessons for about a year, and I picked it up quickly and just loved it. She was afraid I was getting into some bad habits of playing music with my own timing and she wanted me to take formal lessons. So, I was back on Adams Street, this time taking lessons from Mrs. Williams. She lived in another estate home near to Miss Rena's home. Gee-Whiz, I must have been in heaven once again as North Adams Street became a very cultural place for me.

Twice a week I took a walk after school for my piano lessons. Mrs. Williams would first sit me down for cookies and her home brewed sassafras tea, which tasted like warm root beer, a little weird but good. Then she would sternly start my lessons of scales, exercises and basic classical tunes.

Before long with Mother's help also, I was playing some of her favorite tunes and having fun playing with more freedom. Mrs. Williams didn't like that one little bit. She would tap my fingers with a ruler to be sure I held my hands just right. She also had a timing pendulum tick tock back and forth to make me count, count, count and do scales over and over. Boring!

About a year or so of that was enough, so my mother began giving me more lessons herself. At that point, piano playing went from being a bore to being pure joy. Lessons helped, but freedom helped more.

Birthdays were a big deal in our family, after all it was the only day in the year that was just meant for you and for others to help celebrate you.

Mother would bake whatever the birthday boy or girl's favorite cake was. Mine was her made-from-scratch-yellow cake with caramel fudge frosting with pecans, yum. One brother wanted chocolate with chocolate fudge, one yellow with chocolate, and my sister liked a white coconut cake. What a special treat for each of us.

When our father had turned Fifty on January 15, 1954, it was an extra special celebration. He wanted a Devil's food cake with white icing. Our other tradition was having coins in the cake for the age, in Daddy's case he would have one big 50-cent piece. After the wishes and candles were blown out, Mama would cut the cake for the person to have the first piece. It was always fun watching them take a bite and then oops, what was in the cake I wonder? A little coin or coins neatly wrapped in wax paper. The previous year Daddy had a quarter, two dimes and four pennies, a big bite for sure!

It had always been a mystery to me as to how Mama achieved this miracle of that first slice being the exact piece with the coins. She always got the right slice, every time. It took a while for me to learn this secret trick. After wrapping the coins, Mama would lay it on top of the iced first layer, then the top layer and icing hid that treasure. The trick was that she put a piece of scotch tape under the plate to mark the position. We would watch her turn that cake around and smile as she cut the exact piece. She was sly, fun, and brought joy to our birthday celebrations.

The next year I was turning Twelve on December 18, 1955. To my surprised, my parents let me have an actual birthday party with girls *and boys*!

Only a few of each maybe ten kids in all, but that was a tough choice because I had acquired a lot of friends by then.

George and Shay helped me with the guest list, and we managed to get it down to just ten. I felt sad about not being able to include more of my classmates. But we had time to get together as we worked our way to High School. There would be lots of dances and proms for everyone to enjoy.

I had a fairly good stack of 45-rpm records to play on our new hi-fi console. Mother made a big bowl of punch with Lime Sherbet and Ginger Ale with Maraschino cherries floating on top, so delicious and pretty. We had Mama's chocolate chip cookies, bowls of nuts, little triangle sandwiches, lots of potato chips and onion dip and of course ice cream. Mother made my favorite cake topped with toasted pecan halves. I wondered if there would be a dime and two pennies or two nickels and two pennies in my slice of cake.

Since we all had taken our classes in Charm, Manners, Dancing, and Etiquette, everyone behaved pretty well, and we actually danced. Not the box step though, rock and roll required fast jitterbug dancing, and just a few slow dances. The Hokey Pokey and Bunny Hop made us laugh when we messed up the steps, but it all was glorious and perfect.

Being twelve was a big deal for me and having that special party with boys and girls was the best gift my parents could have given me. Wonder if this will ever happen again for another birthday?

I could dance, had manners, was charming and played the piano. What culture I was gaining.

Fifth Avenue Elementary

1955-1956 6th Grade

Mrs. Sustar, Our Teacher

Dance and Music in the '50s

Jitterbug • Boogie Woogie • Be-Bop • Hand Jive • Bunny Hop • Cha
Chalypso • The Stroll • Line Dancing • Lindy Hop • Rock n' Roll • Jive
Swing Dancing • And of Course Slow Dancing • The Hokey Pokey
The Bunny Hop

A Short List of Hit Songs

Do You Want to Dance Bobby - Freeman • Ain't That a Shame - Fats
Domino • Heartbreak HotelElvis Presley • The Purple People Eater
Sheb Wooley • Return To MeDean Martin • Rock 'N' Roll Music Chuck
Berry • The Twelfth of NeverJohnny Mathis • All I have to Do is Dream.
The Everly Brothers • True Love WaysBuddy Holly • Twilight Time The
Platters • The Great Pretender The Platters • Too Marvelous for Words
- Frank Sinatra • Bye-Bye Love - The Everly Brothers • A Teenager in
LoveDion & The Belmonts • Maybelline - Chuck Berry • Little Darlin'
The Diamonds • Rock And Roll Is Here to Stay • Danny & The Juniors
It's Only Make-Believe - Conway Twitty • Loving You - Elvis Presley
Cherry Pink and Apple Blossom - Perez Prado • Love Is a Many-Splendored
Thing - Four Aces. • Do You Want to Dance - Bobby Freeman Ain't That a
Shame Fats Domino • Heartbreak Hotel Elvis- Presley • The Purple People
Eater - Sheb Wooley • Return to Me - Dean Martin • Rock 'N' Roll Music
Chuck Berry • The Twelfth of Never Johnny Mathis • All I have to Do is
Dream. The Everly Brothers • True Love Ways - Buddy Holly Twilight Time
- The Platters

CHAPTER TWENTY-THREE

Nature is Pandora's Box

Was it me who said, when I was younger, that I wanted to have curves when I was older? Yeah, well I liked them when I looked in the mirror, but I sure did *not* like the way the boys looked at all the girls at school. What was wrong with them anyway? They don't bother me so much, but they sure do pester the girls who have bigger curves than I have. That seemed to be the majority of the girls, not me.

Time seemed to have passed too quickly up to this point. Our third grade had moved up to the fourth with Mrs. Faulkner. She was a sweet lady and wonderful teacher who we all liked. She let us have parties now and then, even cookouts at her house. The fifth grade brought a lot of changes and harder studies. Mrs. Patterson made the lessons more challenging for us, but I liked that. How fortunate we were to have these teachers at Fifth Avenue Elementary.

We also helped plan and stage some plays in the auditorium. That was the most fun of all to me. It was great watching the guys at recess getting better and better at their ballgames, especially football. The girls loved the May Pole Dance with the pretty ribbons, and the Virginia Reel, and sometimes even Square Dancing. The boys moped and grumbled, the girls laughed and danced. It was all fun.

By the time sixth grade with Mrs. Sustar rolled around, it seemed the whole class looked a little different and even had different attitudes, some good some not so good. The first thing we all noticed was that since the girls were finally *all changing* from straight up and down to curves here and there, new clothing and undergarments were needed.

That particular change in my curves required a very embarrassing trip with my mother to buy my first brassiere; oh, I can hardly even write that word. I think my head hung down the whole time we were in Belk Gallants as the chirpy saleslady smiled that knowing smile and nodded her head. Then she took out a tape measure right there in the store and measured my chest. Right there for all to see!

With her smug smile she pulled out the *perfect* training under garment for a beginner. *Training*, what was involved with training? My brothers were already teasing me and now I had to train them, will the humiliation never end?

The final choice was mostly a garment that looked virtually flat in the front and hooked in the back. However, it achieved the purpose Mother and I both wanted, nothing showed under my blouses or sweaters now. I didn't have to hold my books close to my chest or keep my arms crossed most of the time. I could jump rope and play softball and stuff without worrying about those sore things on my chest that were not trained yet.

There was a huge difference in the boys from who they were as eight-year-olds when they were sweet, fun, easy to talk with, and even acted shy at times. They had morphed into whole new creatures when they turned twelve. Most of the boys were dressing a little sharper and taking care to comb their hair, some too much care. They constantly combed their hair or tried to keep their unkempt hair looking neater. Combs were then stuck in the hip pocket of their denim jeans.

Also, there was a definite shift in the grouping of boys into those that wore their shirt sleeves rolled up, blue jeans cuffed just so, and wearing black high topped Converse tennis shoes. These guys also developed a slower paced swagger that looked kind of swell on them, it gave them a sense of confidence.

Blake McCloud had developed that cool swagger ahead of most of the other boys in our class. *I noticed.*

Then there were always the nice boys who dressed well. They wore slacks with belts, shirts were tucked in, and always had neatly combed hair with a perfect part. Some put so much wax in their hair that even a strong wind could not shift one hair. But they looked cute and nice.

Now the girls who had *bumped out* earlier than most of us had already taken on flirty ways. And the boys congregated around those girls like bees to a honeybee hive. Those girls also had hips that were round enough to sway. It was hard to move your hips when you were straight up and down.

As time progressed it appeared that my body parts rounded also, the hip thing was not going to be a problem for me. I was blessed with what they called a pear shape at this point in my growing life. And that is all I am going to say about that. I was trying to learn to move my hips a bit, not too much, just a bit.

But then when the rest of us girls started getting our shapes and wearing tighter clothes, those same beehive boys began to move in our direction. Yeah, changes made a difference. *Buzz, Buzz.*

I do not know why my body did this, but when a cute guy talked to me, I found I was slightly swaying and playing with my hair. More and more of these uncontrollable mannerisms seemed to go throughout the whole sixth grade. Mrs. Sustar had her hands full trying to keep all of us paying any attention to what she was teaching. Lots of fidgeting ensued.

There were, of course, the actions of boys that were definitely controlled and very irritating. If a boy sat behind a girl in the classroom, or the cafeteria, or the auditorium they loved to reach over and pop the elastic on the girl's bra. What in the heck was wrong with them? Then after school they would congregate like a pack of wolves waiting to jump on their prey, *us girls.*

I have to admit that most of us did not move away from that wolf pack and that was a bit of a mystery to me. We all seemed to like the attention even though sometimes they could irritate us. It would seem these guys we have known for so long became a little more interesting or more fun to talk to somehow. It all was a bit mysterious and unexplainable.

The nice girls should have avoided the *wolf pack*, we surely knew better. Even though I knew it was those nice boys behaving in a normal fashion who I should have hung around, the wolf pack was more interesting me. I must admit that when one of those *wolf boys* looked directly at me and gave me a big wink, I blushed and got warm all over.

Stop that, Judy, what is wrong with you? And would I look back at him again? Yes. Holy Cow I think all of us were becoming slaves to our uncontrollable bodies. I had to get more information on this whole new phenomenon. *Mother can help, she knew everything.*

Was my brain listening to my mouth when I said to ask Mama? Well, that started the beginning of a new era in things I wish I had never asked about and never wanted to know. If only I could have known what the answers were going to be, for sure I never ever would have asked.

Now maybe I should have just talked to the older girls as we sat discussing everything on the hill. They acted all smarty and wise about life. *They would have known all the answers for sure.*

When I just made one small comment to Mama, I opened Pandora's Box. I read a lot of different books and that happened to be in one of the stories, so I understood what that term meant. Keep it closed, tightly. *Do Not Open Pandora's Box of Temptations!*

"Mama, the boys at school are acting all strange and different this year, like they are not the same boys or something," I innocently said to my Mama that day after school, while she was doing some darning and sewing.

She laid down her sewing and patted the seat by her on the sofa for me to sit down. Oh no, I had to sit close, so she is going to see my red face, "Give me some examples of what they are doing."

"Well, like today the boy behind me reached over and pulled on my bra strap but I pulled away from him. It really embarrassed me," I began.

"Now Judy, it wasn't that nice George Mitchell, was it?" she suddenly asked.

"Golly no, he would never do that," I quickly said, but thought to myself, *hmm, would he ever do that?*

Continuing my conversation, I commented, "Then outside of school some of the wilder boys were flirting and winking and making me really blush and I got warm all over. It was a very strange feeling."

Oh no, as usual I was blurting out more than I intended. *Stop blathering out everything, Judy.* And yet I continued to tell her more very quickly, afraid she would stop me and want more details. She didn't.

"I see. And I suppose last year these same boys were not doing or saying things that embarrassed you?" she asked calmly.

"No, they were my nice, sweet guys that I have known since third grade. I do admit a lot of us girls look different since we are starting to get figures. My hips are rounder, too rounded I think, and I actually have a waistline," I explained all this as if she did not already know how I looked.

To myself I was thinking that the best benefit is that I no longer needed a training bra; *guess they learned their lessons on their own.* I now filled out a larger bra and felt more comfortable in my new clothes.

Hey, I will try a subject changer, "Oh, Mama, I just love the new clothes you made me and the sweaters that Patsy knitted." Yeah, she knew I was changing the subject, but I kept talking. "I feel so grown up now. And since you let me wear those little pink heels to church, I feel even more grown. Thank You."

"Of course, Honey, I love making clothes for you and the new styles are really a lot of fun to sew. I am glad you appreciate my work," she said and patted my hand.

Honey, did she call me Honey? Oh boy, what does that mean? I'll bet she wants to tell me something really important, I thought to myself.

"Well, this is as good a time as any to talk to you about something personal. Your brothers are out for a while and Daddy's at work, so we are alone. You definitely need to hear some details about boys and girls."

My mind was thinking, *Oh Boy, Oh no, close that Pandora's Box!* I have done it now. I am not going to like what she is going to tell me. But I listened anyway.

"You are a very bright girl and I know you will understand these things, these natural things, very easily," she began.

All I could do was think to myself loudly, *No, I'm not bright. You should see my longhand all stingy and running off the blackboard. I won't understand, I don't want to hear anything more.*

"You know we had a movie in class about marriage, and then children came along, and we should all be careful about our feelings until we want to marry someone." I intentionally said this rapidly aloud as if this explained everything that needed to be explained.

"Yes, I have seen that little movie the school considers will prepare you children for life, it does not. You probably didn't learn anything you didn't already know and understand, right?"

"Yes, ma'am, it was a really dumb movie. We all laughed," I told her hesitantly.

Now there I was hearing the *facts of life*, told to me in ways that I would or could not fully comprehend or understand. Mother had been a schoolteacher, so she used a lot of literal and real terms and vivid images.

Oh, the images. Stop, wait a minute now. I don't want to know bedroom stuff, oh now I will never be able to pass their closed bedroom door again.

Nor do I want to know why boys are built different from girls and what those awful boys would do to us sweet girls. What are those *hormones* she keeps talking about, like they were a curse or something?

I thought when I had my first kiss it would be the biggest thing that ever would happen in my life. Now she tells me I have *all that* to look forward to in the future. Was God making a joke when he made us girls go through what we do and what boys do and all that. And where does this *Love* come in?

Oh Lord, help me understand. My eyes must have been bulging out of my head because my mother picked up my hand and held it in her two hands. That was a comforting thing she did that always worked to calm me down.

"Why, Judy, you are shaking. Are you alright? Perhaps I told you too much too soon. I always expect so much out of you because you act older than your twelve years. But these are different and real facts." She told me in her soothing voice.

"Tell you what let's do. You go in there are get one of those warm chocolate chip cookies I just made. And I think we have covered enough for now. Is that all right, Honey?"

I muttered, "Yes ma'am," but at once bolted out the front door. How could I keep a cookie down when my stomach was doing somersaults? Oh *gag*, *gag*, I am never getting married. If that is what has to happen for you to make babies, then I just won't have any children. I will enjoy my nephews and nieces. And she said there was more to learn, good grief!

I was walking quite fast down Adams Street with my head down, muttering unintelligible words, and shaking my head. Suddenly, I came to an abrupt halt when my friend Billy had to swerve on his bicycle to avoid hitting me.

"Gosh, Judy, I am so sorry, are you alright? I didn't mean to come so close to you, but you were moving like a locomotive," he joked.

Not a boy, anybody but a boy, any other time, and not a cute boy like Billy Bridges. What is happening to me? My world is upside down. Evidently my face was beet red, so Billy was a little concerned about me. He was one of the nice boys, but he was still a boy. I could not look him in the face.

"Can I take you home on the back of my bike?" That nice Billy offered.

All I could think was, *You want me to sit on the back of your bike?* You want me to be close to you with my arms around you to hold on. Oh no, buddy-boy, I am not going to fall for that. I will just bet that is how all that stuff starts and I was not going to take a chance of getting into trouble at twelve years of age.

But instead, I muttered, "No, Billy, but thanks." Trying to sound calm I added, "My brothers were just giving me a hard time. You know how they do. I was taking a walk to settle down." Yes, I lied to him.

"Hey Judy, sure I know how that is. As long as you are all right, I'll keep going. See you in school Monday. I think we are going to do the Virginia Reel that day. I like to do that dance, don't you?" he asked with a smile as if life was just Hunky Dorey.

"Sure, me too," I mumbled. "See you Monday."

I hope I am sick Monday because I do not want to dance the *Virginia Reel* and hold hands with all those boys. Looking back, I saw Bill peddling away and he turned around with a big grin and gave me a wave.

Of course, I waved back and smiled a little. Gosh he sure was nice and that was so sweet to worry about me. Maybe I just needed to sort things out. There are just too many cute boys. Mama said I was smart, so I was going to use my smarts and get a handle on this boy and girl stuff.

Just the good parts, maybe, and not try to learn to much too fast, that should work.

CHAPTER TWENTY-FOUR

Elementary Ends then Blends

Our walk to school that day went along as usual, with Shay, Betty, Cynthia, Neal, George, and friends joining us along the way. We were chatting and gossiping as six graders do, enjoying the Springtime blooms, soon to be going into Summertime fun. We had no clue what that day was about to bring us.

Shay was her usual pretty and happy self with her brown hair perfectly turned under. We carried on our easy conversations. We could talk about anything and everything from giggles and wiggles, fears, and tears, to our many days of fun in the sun.

She had been my best friend since I started third grade at Fifth Avenue Elementary. Here we were at the end of the sixth grade, still fast friends and fortunate enough to have gathered a wonderful group of true friends in those four years together.

We all noisily settled in at our desks and finally quieted down. Mrs. Sustar started to run her eyes over the whole classroom, not saying a word. Was this a good or bad thing?

"Students, I have some important things to tell you today so listen carefully please," she said rather slowly and quietly. It was a little scary. "As many of you know a new school has been built on McDonough Street just beyond McKoy park," she continued.

Most of us were aware of this new school as we had watched it being built while sitting on the clay bank just beyond the tennis courts. Yeah, we were curious about what that meant to us.

"Well, some of you will be going to College Heights for your seventh year." We were looking around in a bit of a panic. What did the word *some* mean?

"Those of you who live beyond East Lake Drive will be attending the new school. That is not quite half of you students." She paused and waited, knowing how we would react.

A wave of comments covered the classroom like a chilly blanket. After the groans lessened, Mrs. Sustar went on, "That of course, means you will be the first seventh grade class in the new school to hold your graduation there."

All right, that will be fun maybe. I had already been trying to think of who would be going there with Shay and me. Let's see, Billy, Neal, Gail, ...

She had begun talking again, "After that one year, you will all be going to the eighth grade at Decatur High School. Then you will be in the same school with your friends once more."

We had all been waiting for that day to come. Nirvana, heaven, sunshine and light must be in that High School. That also must mean we would not have Mrs. Selfridge as our teacher. It had to be a gift to have a new school and a new teacher and be the senior class of the new school. Life was looking better.

Evidently, teachers can hear whispers, see notes being passed, catch someone looking at their classmate's test, and mostly pick up on any rumor that trickles throughout the classroom.

Mrs. Sustar was watching and listening, "In case you all are wondering what your teacher's name is for next year, let me tell you that there is a new teacher joining us at Fifth Avenue Elementary."

After allowing that to sink in a bit, she added, "Now there is one last bit of news for you to absorb hopefully in a grown-up fashion. Our own seventh grade teacher, Mrs. Selfridge has been assigned to College Heights, so half of you will have her as your teacher." And she waited.

This news left a complete silence at first in the classroom. We had heard she was a tough teacher, so we were all thinking about this. We were being split up which was not cool at all, and now half of us will have her as our teacher, not a new one.

My brother Tommy really liked Mrs. Selfridge. In fact, I remember him telling me not to listen to kids and make up my own mind when she was my teacher. I listened to my brother most of the time, so I would do just that. It might be a good thing after all.

Then I looked over at George. He caught my eye and frowned. We both put our hands up in a *what's going to happen now* motion. It would not be good.

There continued to be a lot of *oh no's* and *aw geezes*, and *shucks* went around the room. More muttering went throughout the sixth-grade class. *Split up, what's with that, anyway?* What does that mean for half of us? Oops, we must have been too loud for that news.

Mrs. Sustar rapped the ruler decisively on her desk and continued, "Now class, you have to settle down and listen to me. There are a lot of changes for all of you next year. Seventh grade is a wonderful time because you will have more responsibilities and the lower classes will be looking at you to know how to act. You will each be a role model to the younger students."

Some of the boys clapped their hands over their mouths to keep from laughing out loud. *Us acting as role models? What does that even mean?* Those sorts of comments and such rippled throughout.

We all started looking around wide eyed and shaking our heads and the boys groaned. Boys had no manners; they always groaned about everything. The girls were quiet but thinking.

"Would you like to hear some good news?" she asked. Our wide-eyed expectant faces answered her.

"Since this was a big year, we wanted to give you a party, a swimming party at maybe Lake Winfield Scott." Smiles replaced the frowns.

"I realize half of you will not be here to graduate with the rest of your friends at this school and I truly want all of you to have a good time together. I suppose in a way this will be a going away party," she told us.

"But just think boys and girls, in just one year you will all be back together when you graduate and move up to the eighth grade at Decatur High School. That will be a big move for all of you!" Mrs. Sustar then gave us one of her big caring smiles, making everything seem right.

That possibly could have been the best idea any teacher ever had. She arranged for a bus to take us to the lake. There were picnic tables, sandy beaches, a concession stand with lockers and rooms for us to change into our bathing suits. They had arranged to have hot dogs, hamburgers, potato chips, cookies, and lots of goodies that kids our age constantly snacked on.

At first the boys and girls stayed on their own area of the beach. Then those hormone things Mother had told me about kicked in and the boys moved like a herd of cattle all at once over to the girls. I would love to have known which boy instigated that ingenious plan. It worked because we all had fun. Someone had bought a portable radio, so they played some rock and roll music.

You know, our class was full of personalities some good, some quiet, some funny, some smart, some pretty, and some were cute. Yet we all came together to form a pretty dynamic class. Now it was breaking up for a year, but High School would bring us back together once more.

Our days at Fifth Avenue had ended, but we were now blending into our new school. My seventh grade at the new College Heights School was quite different than I had expected it to be. We were the *older class* now and were on a *buddy plan* to the first graders to help them and be their friend.

The biggest change I was realizing was this became my transition year. Several things led up to that conclusion. The first most pleasant surprise everyone had was how much we learned from Mrs. Selfridge. Those girls so long ago truly had made exaggerations, for she was a terrific and caring teacher.

Tommy was exactly right telling me to wait until I had her as my own teacher before judging her, wise brother. She was strict, but we needed that many times, so it was all right. She also worked with us individually and we knew she really cared for us, very cool of her.

The second much more difficult thing for me to realize was that I no longer would have my friend George in my class. Not just that he wouldn't be in my class, but Dr. Mitchell was moving his practice across town. That meant we were losing our Family Doctor and I was losing my classmate, my boyfriend, my pal for the last four terrific years. Also, half of my schoolmates were not in my class, and this all added up to make me very sad.

The third transition was a good one. I was meeting new friends and widening my scope of friends as they all lived on or beyond McDonough. I was having get-togethers, sleepovers, and parties in a new territory. Again, this was preparing me for High School where student would come from all sides of Decatur. Some transitions can be good ones.

I had been on the patrols for several years at Fifth Avenue and helped raise the flag each morning. We all said the Pledge of Allegiance with great respect and patriotism. After taking the flag down in the evening, we folded it into a perfect triangle handling it carefully so as not to touch the ground. It was an honor that I truly cherished.

Now I was the Captain of the Patrols at College Heights, making me happy. I made sure my badge and straps were bright, clean, and shiny.

It was wonderful that Shay was with me for that seventh-grade school year. She was like my home base. We all did meet many new people and started new circles of friends. Billie Gae Selman, Jeanne Bellville, and Janet Blalock to name a few, became good friends. We had sleepovers and parties with boys being around to make things even more fun. Yes, it was all right being right where we were right then.

FIFTH AVENUE   MARCH 1957

We all liked being in the brand-new shiny school. This was also the time in my life that things were changing in my body as it was with many of my classmates. We were feeling and experiencing more *grown-up* things. At times this was all right, but other times it was too emotional, too painful, and too perplexing to handle. My emotions were happy, then really sad. I cried too easily and got my feelings hurt too much. I worked on those problems, I truly tried.

My brothers took these changes in my mood and body worse than I did. They were used to having a little *bratty sister* to pick on and tease, but now they hesitated to punch or pick on me as much. Wow, there was one terrific plus to becoming a teenager. Was more good news in store for me? Ending then blending was cool after all.

Ending and Blending can be good, and more adventures and fun was in store along the way.

CHAPTER TWENTY-FIVE

Friendship, Scouting, and Outings

There was one enduring fact in my life, my friendship with Shay. That friendship carried me through a lot of tough teen times. I was fortunate to have great friends at school and in our neighborhood, but having a best friend was a gift. We could be around each other and feel comfortable, never having to act differently than we really felt that day.

Sharing the activities, catching one another's jokes, and getting over those rare silly spats quickly were traits of our friendship. We especially needed each other during all those new changes in our life because being a teenager was tough enough alone.

Our neighborhood had many homes with lots of kids for instant playmates. Of course, the best part was living next to McKoy Park with its skating oval, playground, a greenhouse for summer projects, tennis courts, ball fields and best of all a pool.

Yes, we went to school together, but the most fun was had during the summer. We rode our bicycles further than we should have, swam and sunbathed at any pool, lake, river or creek we could. We would spend the night at one or the other's house at a moment's notice. My little bag was always ready with PJs, toothbrush, hairbrush, and a change of clothes.

We had fun with our school friends and seemed to have several boyfriends here and there. We had dance parties, outdoor parties, and lake outings. Some classmates had dance parties at their homes. Having get-togethers, sleepovers, and many trips to any body of water, kept us busy during the summers.

One day I had some exciting news to share. "Hey Shay, if we join the Girl Scouts did you know we get to go to a two-week camp in North Georgia?"

"You, mean we get to go away without our parents, or my sisters, or your brothers, or anybody?" Shay replied with a bit of a giggle in her voice.

Happy to hear she liked the idea, I continued, "Yep, just us and who-ever else decided to join from our class. But we will meet a lot of new people and I think we sleep in tents. I love sleeping in tents, don't you?"

She laughed and said, "Well, since we sleep in your tent in your back-yard so much, we will have some advantages, don't you think?"

"Yeah, but the best part will be that we won't have my two brothers poking around on the tent with sticks to scare us or turning the hose onto the tent to make us think it is raining."

We both laughed because we always knew they would pull stunts like that, so we screamed and yelled at the appropriate times. Sure, enough you could hear them laughing and hooting. It prepared us quite well.

When the time came to pack for our Girl Scout Camp trip, there had been a strict list of what clothes to bring. Mostly shorts, tops, swimsuits, sneakers and lots of bug spray and sunburn lotion. We laughed reading the list.

"Okay, we will just empty the drawers of our chest of our summer wear, and we are all set!" Shay said.

Being the ever-watchful Mother, my Mama checked each piece of clothing to stitch up any tears or holes. She carefully sewed on *This belongs to Judy Reach* on every single piece. The tags in the panties scratched like crazy, but I wasn't about to say anything to her. I really appreciated how she cared for my clothes and for me.

The timing of this camping trip was perfect because I needed a break from my family. They would appreciate a break from me too. It just seemed everyone drove me nuts those days. They treated me like I didn't know any-thing or like I was a kid or something.

I was thirteen, are they kidding, I was a teenager, and they were trying to tell me how to do and say things? No, I didn't like that one bit. In fact, my mother would repeat many times the phrase, "Oh, yes, I forgot, you know everything now, don't you, Judy?"

What was I supposed to say? I usually crossed my arms stubbornly, but to myself I thought, well yeah, I guess I do know about everything. Kenny and Tommy have been telling me stuff for a long time, and they really did know everything, or at least that is what I was told.

Being a teenager was something I had been looking forward to for a long time. Now it seemed thirteen was just one more birthday. Yeah, I needed a new outlook and a new adventure.

For example, one morning I woke up, made the bed, and walked past my mirror. "Holy Cow, what is that? I said aloud. Well, Tommy was walking by in the hall, so I asked him for help.

"Look Tommy, I have a wart on my face!" I whispered loudly, not wanting anyone else to hear.

Naturally Tommy laughed, "That is not a wart, it is a pimple."

"A pimple, oh no Buddy Boy, I do not get pimples, maybe it's a pink bubble or something."

"Call it anything you want, but it is still a pimple," he said flatly.

He held up his hand saying to wait a second. After rummaging in the drawers of mystery that I was never allowed to look into, or even walking near their bedroom was an offense.

"Here, put this on that bump to cover it and help it heal. Keep it, I have another one," and with a smug smirk he left.

Ugh, it stunk, but I put some on that wart-red-bubble-pimple thing anyway. Hmm, it did look better, so maybe I could go to school after all that day. At school I held a book in front of my face to hide the throbbing thing on my cheek. Looking around at other kids I notice several had the same affliction. Was it catching, like the measles? I made it through that day and the offending bump did start to heal. Guess I would live, but that stinky tube was always with me everywhere.

Back to our camp packing, we had all our clothes neatly folded and cleaned and our sneakers were perfectly white. We even bought our bottle of shoe whitener just in case the sneakers got scuffed. I am not sure why we thought we would need that, since we would be in tents, on top of dirt, walking and sitting on dirt. Who knew what was ahead of us in those wild mountains, forests, and lakes?

The bus ride with the other Girl Scouts was a lot of fun as we met the new kids and felt freer already. As we rode higher into the North Georgia Mountains the scenery was even more gorgeous. There were dense forests, rapid creeks, steep inclines, and ears popping from the altitude change.

Shay and I had been on trips in the mountains with Mama and Daddy, like Vogel State Park, Lake Hiawassee, and Brasstown Bald, the highest point in Georgia. Shay's family had taken us water skiing on Lake Lanier, great, great fun.

With my parents, we visited and stayed a night or two in some quaint North Georgia Mountain areas like Helen, Toccoa Falls, Tallulah Gorge, and my favorite, Dahlonega. That was where horse drawn buggies filled with gold mined from the area had been taken to Atlanta. That precious gold went on the State Capitol Dome, the shiny bright gold dome.

This trip was entirely different, we were sort of on our own. We were feeling independent for sure. Hey, we were well travelled and prepared for this two-week jaunt. This time there were no parents, let freedom ring. What did we have in store for us in the next two weeks?

When we finally arrived at Camp Winona, it was even more beautiful than we had imagined. Our tent was large and on a concrete platform, no rain could seep, creep or drip in there. The side flaps could roll up, so it was nice and cheerful. There were four beds to a tent, and we were expected to have our bed made and tucked perfectly tight in the morning with all our stuff stowed away neatly, they checked! I forgot one day and had to run lickity split back to straighten up my area. I made it before they checked our tent. Whew!

We learned something new every day like, canoeing and capsizing canoes fully dressed, when I lost one of my white sneakers! We rode horses, learned how to start and tend a fire, and how to be more self-reliant. Anybody who knew me knew I never liked messes, so wouldn't you know we had to learn to dig our own latrine. Fortunately, they had supplied portable toilets for us.

We went on many hikes and one long hike to a mountain top. We were well prepared for the steep rocky trails after climbing Stone Mountain many times. The first week it was let freedom ring and Yippee-yi- yo-ki-yay, we were far away. Then the second week became harder because it was not always easy and we did get a little homesick, maybe a lot homesick.

The counselors kept us quite busy and organized, so there was not a lot of time to be alone. They also provided a little outdoor store where we could buy necessities like combs, toothbrushes, and postcards. We were supposed to write home every other day on of those cards. I mostly did that.

Shay and I had an exciting time and the two girls in our tent were very cute and kind of nice. We sat around a big bonfire at night making 'smores where the leaders told ghost stories or let us know about upcoming projects. One of those projects was putting on a play in the mess hall that we put together ourselves, fun. Oh, yes, and the food was great.

Having Shay with me was a lot of comfort because there were new and scary experiences. It was good for us to stretch ourselves by going to that camp. We did well but we were ready to go home. I didn't tell anybody that, nope that was for me and Shay to share.

Girl Scout Camp was a good summertime experience. It also would help us be prepared for High School that very same year of 1957. Shay and I were a little battered and bruised, but it was fun and was a good learning experience to be a little bit on our own.

You would never believe it, but we returned home with the white sneaker polish untouched.

Stone Mountain carving

CHAPTER TWENTY-SIX

Yarns about Yarn

Just as Daddy had done many times, Patsy was doing full time, taking the trolley downtown to work. They were on different trolleys though. To pass the time as she made her way to and from work every day, she took up knitting. Patsy became an adept knitter quickly. She was exceptionally good with any type of needle just like Mama. And just like Mama, she did not like her hands to be idle.

The most fascinating projects Patsy worked on were the colorful argyle socks, which required five or six bobbins of a variety of colored yarns to dangle as she wove the intricate patterns. Those colorful bobbins danced and bobbed the faster she knitted. She created many of the designs herself. You can be sure all the males in our family were able to wear fancy warm argyle socks.

On one of her daily commutes, she was surprised to hear someone saying something to her, very unusual on these rides. "Pardon me, Miss, but I have been watching you knit on this trolley for a long time. I always knew when you were knitting socks, they were easy to spot." This remark came from the gentleman sitting across from her on the trolley car.

Patsy had seen him and many of the same people each day, but rarely did anyone talk to their fellow passengers. Most read their newspapers.

He cleared his voice as if he might have appeared rude to just blurt that out to her. But he continued, "Well this new project you have started has me puzzled. You are knitting with only one color, red. It has gotten too big to be socks." He seemed truly mystified. "Then I started wondering if it was a sweater, but now it looks too long to fit anyone."

Suddenly a woman's voice chimed in, "Oh, I think it is a very large red scarf that would be quite warm."

Her friend said, "Yes, we have had many discussions about what you are making with that lovely yarn. It has been weeks that you have been working on that one project. It is a sweater coat, isn't it? She inquired.

Patsy had a sly sense of humor and liked to pull people's legs now and then. She said in a serious voice, "To tell you the truth before I started the project, I bought too much of this red yarn. So now I am making something, but don't know exactly what it will end up being."

Everyone looked startled that she would spend such an enormous amount of time knitting on something that she had no idea what it would turn out to be.

"If you would like we will all just wait and see what it shapes up to be in a couple of weeks." The fellow commuters looked at one another with a bit of bewilderment. But they agreed to wait to see her finished work.

Patsy still heard whispers like, "It's a blanket for sure. See how long it is?"

"No, I think it is a very fancy shawl with all that beautiful cable work she is doing."

They waited and watched.

Then the day came when my petite sister boarded the trolley looking exceptionally striking. Heads turned as she walked down the aisle in her shiny black heels, black purse, and a strand of pearls at her neck wearing an exquisite red dress with intricate cabled designs.

She had no knitting bag with her, and the fellow travelers were making quiet remarks to one another. "She looks very chic and classy, don't you think?" And "She is lovely today, isn't she?"

The gentleman who first began talking to Patsy, tipped his hat at her and sat silently enjoying the delightful new look of his fellow traveler.

Finally, a lady said, "Excuse me, but we have waited patiently to see that project finished and here you come today with no knitting bag and no yarn."

Another asked, "Did you give up on the knitting because you could not decide how to finish it? It was getting to be a big piece, wasn't it?"

Without a word Patsy stood up while the trolley was still stopped. She made a nice little twirl and said to all, "This is it."

There was a unified gasp. "Do you mean you have been knitting that lovely dress all this time?"

Patsy started giggling with her contagious laughter, "Yes, I was making this cabled dress the whole time and it had to be a surprise. So, Surprise!"

After they finally realized her little trick, they all laughed. Then they complimented her and told her how beautiful the dress looked and how pretty she looked wearing it.

Patsy had pulled off a good joke on her fellow commuters. They were now friends.

However, when she had taken her knitting project with her on one of our family rides one day, things went quite differently. As usual Mama was in the front seat nestled right next to Daddy as he drove. Kenny sat in front by the window, leaving Tommy, Patsy, and me in the back seat.

Now Tommy was just the sweetest guy ever, he really was, but he did have a little mischief in him. He started watching Patsy's hands deftly clicking away with the needles and that red yarn and got a twinkle in his eye.

Maybe he became mesmerized by her swiftly moving hands and her shiny knitting needles. Tommy rubbed his chin and began to have a bright idea. He whispered quietly to me "Wouldn't it be fun to toss that big ball of yarn out the open window and see what happens?"

Before I could tell him, "Maybe you shouldn't do that, Tommy" he had acted on his idea.

Perhaps this was a misguided thought. Having the mentality of his fourteen years, he grabbed the big round ball of red yarn and did just that. Out the open window it flew.

To his horror and Patsy's surprise, the yarn immediately began unraveling. Daddy kept driving down the road not knowing what had taken place in the back seat.

"EEK! My yarn, it's disappearing." Patsy squealed. At that moment her hand jerked as the yarn began to quickly unravel her knitting.

It was then that she yelled and believe you me, she could give a loud yell. "Stop the car, Please, Stop!"

Daddy screeched to a halt causing all of us to lurch forward.

Then he very sternly asked, "What in the Good Lord's Name has happened now? What are you all doing back there?"

Mother gave him an elbow to the ribs for cursing. Kenny immediately whipped his head around to see what was wrong in the back seat. He was glad it wouldn't be him this time.

Then Daddy comprehended what had happened and checked to see if we had recovered from being thrown swiftly forward into the back of the front seat. No problem, we were tough and wanted to see what was happening with Tommy.

Tommy didn't get into trouble very often, so Kenny was smiling in satisfaction. He was the first one out to witness the scene of the crime. Then we all climbed out of the car to check on this situation.

To our collective amazement we were staring at a long red zigzag line. The red line trailed back along the side of the road as far as the eye could see.

Patsy looked at Tommy with such a glare that without her having to say one word, he knew what he had to do to try to make this right. He immediately started rolling the yarn into a ball again. This would take a long time as everyone realized.

As my brother walked and wound, he had to remove grass, sticks, and briars from the yarn. The ball of yarn was already a lot bigger than the one he threw out of the window.

"How did that happen?" he muttered to himself. "And Daddy is probably mad at me for causing such a ruckus and having to slam on the brakes."

"Man, oh Man, I was just trying to have a little fun."

Mother leaned against the car while she made a tsk-tsk noise with her tongue and kept shaking her head.

Meanwhile, Kenny was laughing his head off—the only one who laughed by the way. He was holding his stomach because he was laughing so hard. Kenny relished in someone else's punishment or trouble.

"Finally, Tommy did something wrong, not me; and everybody saw it. Man, this is a good one, wait till I tell people about this," Kenny crowed.

At least someone found humor in the disastrous situation.

I had witnessed the entire debacle. When the yarn got unraveled to the point of pulling all the knitted work apart, I knew it was bad, really bad.

I didn't think it was funny that Tommy had done such a crazy thing. Deep in my heart I knew he didn't mean it to happen this way. He was just not that cruel. Kenny was still laughing.

Tommy meanwhile walked and walked and talked to himself with his head hung low.

We could barely hear him mumble, but I know I heard him say, "I thought it would stop. I really did. How was I to know it would keep unraveling?"

Tommy left her knitting alone after that learning lesson. Patsy had to buy more red yarn to match so she could finish her project.

Tommy paid for the yarn with his newspaper delivery money. It was only fair, right?

CHAPTER TWENTY-SEVEN

Ducks, Dogs, and Duck Eggs

When Daddy had to rename our beautiful big Mallard duck from Horace to Hortense when she laid eggs, we knew we had a wonderful unique pet. She loved the little area Daddy had made for her with the sunken tub to splash around in and a doghouse as her home. He had put chicken wire around the area at first to keep her safe, but it became clear that Hortense was a duck that could take care of herself.

When her wing began to heal, she would flutter up and land on anything handy: a branch, a porch rail, a ladder, or any place where she could perch. She loved to be anywhere we were doing some project and would perch, nod her head up and down and make her hissing noise approval. We loved her.

Now that we saw she was healing, we just knew any day she would fly away. When a migrating flock flew over the following year, we were prepared for her to take flight and join them. Hortense stayed and the Reach family was happy. We loved her.

Hortense soon began to fly higher, then to soar as she watched below. That is just how she learned to sense when Daddy would be coming home. She would circle above the trolley stop and slowly fly above the street and above the trees. As Daddy wound his way home on foot Hortense accompanied him in flight. It was truly an amazing sight to watch. Daddy loved it.

The very next season Hortense laid more eggs, this time in a nest she had made in a very inaccessible place, a crawl space right under a chicken coop. Boy Howdy, she knew how to pick a place to nest.

You see our next-door neighbors, the Kimbrell family, owned much of the land surrounding their large white wooden two-story home. Our brick ranch house had been built on the corner lot right next to their house. My friend Carole Kelly's family had the matching brick house as ours on the other side of their big white home.

Before dividing up their land to build a house for their son and one for their daughter, they had horses, large fields, and gardens, and even chickens. All that remained of their farm now was a backyard full of flowers and vegetables and that coop, still full of hens and roosters. In fact, the horses were once on our land, thus our soil was very rich to Mama's delight.

Well, Hortense chose to lay her speckled eggs under that very same chicken coop. Mother seemed to know those eggs had not been fertilized. She also knew that Hortense would continue to sit on her eggs until they hatched, which would be never.

How did Mother know this stuff? She thought up a plan to retrieve those eggs before they began to rot. Ugh. Anyway, she had Tommy keep Hortense otherwise occupied after she finally came out from her dark nesting place. Tommy held her favorite treat in his hand to tempt her to stay outside. She could never pass up dog food pellets. Maybe she had decided she was in fact a dog now.

Tommy got to be the nice guy as usual and make the duck happy. So, what did the last and smallest Reach get to do in this big plan?

Oh sure, retrieve those eggs. Why does it always have to be me? It was bad enough that her nest was underneath a very active coop of hens, but worse to have to crawl through their droppings and stuff. Double Ugh.

Mother gave me a hug and said, "You will do just fine, Judy. You can do this."

Now she knew that was not true because she knew everything. Also, it was Mama who named me Miss Nasty Nice. She said I was just too nice to be around nasty messes and could not stand stinky stuff. It was a correct title.

Usually, I could use my prissy ways to avoid having to deal with such things. So, I tried, "But Mama, it's too stinky, too messy, and too small under there. My clothes will get all messed up and I will get all filthy. And it is dark underneath that scary chicken coop." I pleaded with my best plea; I may have even clasped my hands beneath my chin to plead.

"Judy, I know how kind you are. You would not want Hortense to be sad when those eggs don't hatch into little ducklings, now would you?"

Geeze, see what I mean? You can't win. I did love that duck and knew I had to do this dirty deed, so shimmy and crawl I did. Holding my breath as I pushed along, I tried not to think of what was crunching under my knees. I crawled as quickly as possible through the chicken droppings and loose feathers.

I did it. I retrieved those beautiful big eggs before they spoiled, putting them into my little sack. You never saw anyone crawl backward as fast as I did, even while holding tightly to that sack. I wanted out of there fast.

You know I think I will put this on the list as one of the most unpleasant tasks ever given to me. It was also a sad one, knowing those eggs would never hatch into little Hortense ducklings. I got out of those nasty clothes as fast as possible. Then I took a good, long bath after the ordeal. Nobody better knock on that bathroom door because I was not budging.

Now Kenny and Tommy tried to convince me that after I brought those large eggs to Mother, she had kept them. "Why did she do that?" I inquired.

"Well, you know those nice fluffy scrambled eggs you had this morning?" Kenny said slyly.

"Yes," I hesitantly replied

"Those were Hortense's eggs, and didn't you just enjoy eating them?" Tommy asked, barely hiding his twitching lip. My brothers just loved pulling any joke on me. They stayed outside and watched me run into the house to ask Mother if this was the truth. I was quickly turning a sickly green color. I think I also must have missed hearing their snickers.

"Is it true, Mama, did you cook up our pet duck's eggs and feed them to us?" Tears were welling in my eyes.

Mother wisely smiled down at me and just said, "Now, Judy, don't let those boys tease you so much." Yeah, I saw her look out at my brothers from the window. So, what was the truth?

I think I knew the truth; I trusted my Mama, she loved Hortense.

A few weeks later that Daffy Duck caused more turmoil in our back yard.

"Hey, what is all that commotion outside?" Daddy asked as he threw his newspaper on the floor. "Libby, did you hear that ruckus in the backyard?"

"No telling what it is. It sounds as though some dogs are having a fight. Let me get the boys go see what is happening, Roy."

"Kenny, Tommy, go and see what's going on out there in the back yard," Mother called out to the boys.

I liked to know what the trouble was as long as I was not involved in any way. No repercussions that way.

After discovering the source of the ruckus Mama laughed, "Oh for Heaven's Sake, look at that duck" Mama said as she shook her head at the sight.

"See Libby, she's a great yard protector," Daddy said as they both watched the spectacle in our yard. He was laughing and enjoying the show as they stood safely on the porch

It was our own Hortense protecting our entire back yard. That was one more of her self-imposed duties.

Evidently a couple of dogs dared to climb up the bank of our yard and were about to enter the arena of Hortense. These two trespassers had a surprise in store for themselves.

They did not know they were messing with the Deadly Duck of Spring Street!

She had extended her wonderful wings and was furiously flapping them. She then lowered her head to charge at the interlopers who dared come into her yard. At first the two dogs stopped with dazed looks. What was this vicious animal?

Oh, she was in full attack mode now, as she gained speed. All the while she was loudly sounding her fierce hissing. The dogs began barking. They were bigger after all, but this was a wide and fearsome creature. The closer she came to them the more they began to back up, slowly, slowly, then quickly, quite quickly.

Wising up to the impending danger the pair began whining. Both dogs turned and skedaddled with their tails tucked between their legs, yelping all the while.

What a sight!

Now that the storm was over, Hortense began taming and settling her feathers as she strutted toward Daddy. He was grinning proudly at his great watch duck. She bobbed her head up and down as if tooting her own horn. She accepted his proud pats. Our feathered friend continued to serve our family with faith and diligence

As one would imagine our unusual pet was the talk of the neighborhood. Our friends loved to take pictures with her or admire her feathers. Due to all this attention Hortense had gotten quite vain. She began wiggling and waggling her tail feathers then posed for the snapshot. Smart duck, pretty duck.

Hortense kept her vigilance while being our dearly loved pet until the third migrating season. We had all been prepared for this of course but were saddened to see her looking up and getting fidgety. She paced around in circles, obviously agitated, not knowing what to do.

She looked at us and looked up once more at the V-shaped flock of mallards. With one last look at us, she knew it was more than her instincts could bear. With a hesitant start she began running and soon lifted on her well-mended wings to join the formation.

What a sight, a sad sight for us, but a wonderful life was ahead for our duck returning to her natural habitat. Yes, I cried even though we had all been prepared for this day. She had been strong for a long time. Having lost two sets of eggs was heartbreaking for her and all of us. But she was our pet duck, our watch duck, our Hortense.

Knowing that fact did not keep me from trying to spot her at every park we went to such as Piedmont, or the nearby lakes and ponds. We never spied her and at last accepted the fact that the draw of nature would usually win.

Hortense gave us wonderful memories as she shared her love with us. When we took company to the Cyclorama to see the replica of some battles of the Civil war, one of my favorite places, I would look for her at the lake.

After watching the Elephants for a while, I looked for Hortense among all the ducks. Tommy sat beside me on the bench one time and said, "You know you are not going to find our duck among these ducks, don't you? He quietly asked in his caring brother voice.

"Yeah, I know, Tommy, guess just looking at these ducks reminds me of Hortense. I think she is very happy and that makes me happy. Don't you think she is? Looking up at my brother he just nodded, yes.

What more could any family expect from any pet.

CHAPTER TWENTY-EIGHT

Oh, Brotherhood

Reaches and cars were always a perfect match. All five of us children appreciated the oh-so-wonderful automobile from our early childhood. We learned that love from our Daddy, but for Mother they were merely a mode to get from here to there. No love was involved, just acceptance.

By the time Kenny had his own car, Tommy was working on one for himself. Three cars in the driveway meant a lot of shuffling around. The one in the back had to be moved to allow car one or two to exit the carport and driveway. Tommy and Kenny were very adept at this car shuffling dance.

One day the result of this overcrowding almost caused a disaster. After the careful execution of a three-way switch with the cars, something went awry. We saw the last car start to inch backwards, but there was no driver inside. We realized it was Kenny's car moving down our driveway, our sloping driveway and heading toward the street.

"Oh no, it is headed straight for the Kimbrell's front yard. Do something quick," Mama yelled.

Kenny's famous lightning speed once more came in handy as he raced to his car. He quickly opened the door and slammed on the brakes. It stopped just before hopping the curb into the Kimbrell's yard. It was right in the middle of the street though. Sitting in the line of any car coming down the street either way.

Kenny looked back and forth quickly to be sure no cars were headed towards him, but sure enough, there was one car headed straight at him. Quick action was again required, or disaster would erupt. He got his car started, put it in first gear, drove up and parked it, then firmly set the emergency brake on his cherished automobile.

Kenny was still shaking when he looked up to see it had been his friend and our neighbor Robert Howard's car bearing down on him. Robert smiled, shook his head back and forth, then waved his hand out of the car window. He knew very well about the car situation at the Reach house. It was a close call, but Kenny triumphed.

Kenny's quick reaction came into use not long after that incident. This time averting what could have been a deadly accident. "Help," came a faint cry from outside. Before this plaintive call registered with all of us, Kenny had already shot up from his chair and was racing out of the house to the driveway.

Brothers knew brothers. He knew Tommy was working on his car and could be in trouble. Sure, enough Kenny saw why there had been a call for help. Tommy was wedged under the front of his car as the hitch had begun to slip and was starting to press down on his chest.

Without a moment of hesitation Kenny reached down and somehow lifted the front of that car. He performed this miracle with such ease it amazed all of us as we looked at this sight. Kenny managed to ease that pressure on his brother enough to allow Tommy to scoot himself out from under his car.

"Kenny, Tommy, Oh My Lord, are you hurt?" The anxiety and worry in our mother's voice frightened me. All this drama had happened very quickly.

"Judy, stay here with me out of the way. It looks as if Kenny has saved the day and probably saved his brother," Mama said as she held me close to her.

Daddy reacted with, "That was incredible." He was saying this in almost a daze as we all grasped the gravity of this ordeal. When we saw Tommy shimmy his way from under the car, we all reacted in our own way.

It must have been all that adrenaline pumping through Kenny, for he did not feel any soreness after lifting the car. We were very thankful for Kenny's quick thinking and response. Mother ran to help Tommy to be sure he could stand up. Then she looked at Kenny to see how he was doing after such an unbelievable feat. Kenny was also making sure Tommy was able to breathe and stand.

"Boys, boys, my goodness, my goodness!" Mother was at a loss for words. She was not used to seeing her boys in such a dire situation. That day Kenny acted as a hero for Tommy. His speed, agility, and quick thinking saved his brother. What the next day would hold no one knew.

Daddy was helping everyone now and patting Mama to calm her down. We all sat right down on that driveway trying to get over the commotion. It had all happened quite quickly. I cried of course.

By the time Tommy had turned sixteen and Kenny was eighteen, our brother-sister dynamic had changed. Cars and girls occupied their every spare moment. Since they each had their own cars, both of their cars required constant maintaining of the engine, or waxing, vacuuming, and giving their prized automobiles loving care.

Geeze, they seemed to love their cars more than anything. That is how I thought it was until I discovered they were taking girls out on dates in those gleaming and well-maintained vehicles. Dating girls, where did that leave their little sister?

I was definitely not in their radar range. In addition, all my bruises were healed. Now what was I supposed to do? It was time for me to let them go just a little and be with my own friends. I pouted and moped, and then I perked up when several boys talked to me during recess at school the next day.

Kenny graduated from Decatur High in 1956, when Tommy was a sophomore, and I was still in Elementary School. Changes were going to come once again in my Reach Family, I could feel it.

Then Kenny decided to go to Georgia Tech where our brother Roy had gone, so he stayed home since it was not too far to drive. After a year or so, he got interested in Heating and Air Conditioning and decided to transfer to Georgia Southern. That was when he moved into his own apartment.

There it was another person moving away. Now there was just Tommy and I left. It was very strange not having Kenny around all the time, but he did come up quite often on weekends. I missed Kenny's lightning speed and agility. He and Tommy would have races from the very back of our yard up to the house. Tommy really thought at first that he could ace that foot race, but in this race, they did not run, they walked fast. It was hilarious to see Kenny's determined fast walk with his fast footwork, he beat Tommy by half. Tommy would just give up then we got such a kick out of seeing Kenny doubled over with laughter.

But I already knew a lot about Kenny's super speedy talent. One day we were in the back yard, and I did something to make him really mad, he started running towards me. Well, I sped into the kitchen to my room and locked it quickly. Ah, I made it. Then I heard Kenny running through the Dining Room, Living Room and into the hallway to my other door. Man alive, I barely got across the room to that door to get it locked. There was Kenny banging on my door. How did he do that?

I leaned against that door and sighed in relief. Wait a minute, why was it so quiet? Did he give up on catching me? No, he went out back through the house and out the kitchen door and was coming up the back porch to my door. What? Once again, I just made it as he began pounding on my windows; I quickly closed the blinds. Well, I stayed in my room for a long time, until I heard his car driving away. That was too close, and Kenny was almost too fast that time. Whew!

Kenny's set of wheels when he was sixteen, was a 1946 navy blue Dodge, called the Blue Goose. Daddy said that was the perfect car for him since everyone would know to *dodge* if he was coming!

Our Uncle Foster had helped Kenny get this car, which came with a fascinating history. Uncle Bedford Foster had worked with Daddy in Miami while they were in the Border Patrol. In fact, those two guys met Libby and Muriel Ashley (my mother and her only sister) and they each married those sisters. It is a great family history.

Well, Uncle Foster knew how to deal with and handle situations. They had driven out to a car auction where they sold cars that had been seized in a crime.

Most of these cars had belonged to Bootleggers. Those were the rough and ready group of young guys who hauled illegal moonshine fresh from the Moonshine Still. They raced as fast as their souped-up cars would take them to avoid the law and get the white lightening into the hands of the buyers.

In addition to having large engines, these cars had special springs so the car would not drag the ground when loaded with all those gallon jugs. Before these nefarious characters would haul their illegal whisky, they always removed the back seats to make room for the biggest load possible.

Many of those boys from the swamp and South Georgia ended up driving or working on racecars, even for NASCAR in the late 1940s. This was after they decided to go legal and stay safer, I suppose.

These guys had learned a great deal about how to make any car run fast and stay well-tuned. Breakdowns could cost them dearly and perhaps cause them to be caught by the revenuers, like our Daddy, and land in jail. Those years had taught them a trade they could use after their hooch-running days.

We were not going to get away from those moonshine stills that Daddy had searched for and blown up in the Okefenokee Swamp near Waycross. Yes, the car that Kenny and Uncle Foster had managed to obtain at the auction was indeed one of those bootlegger cars. For the sum of fifty dollars, Kenny knew he had a prize. On the way home from the auction, they stopped at the Lakewood junk yard, found a back seat, installed it, then he proudly drove that blue Dodge home. He now owned his own notorious set of wheels with a shady history, cool.

Kenny and Tommy were well aware of how Mother expected things to stay: clean, neat, tidy and shiny. They had worked on their cars for quick projects in the front yard but went to the back for longer and trickier jobs. When they were finished with their chore it was expected that they would pick everything up and put it away so that the front of the house always looked nice.

In fact, our carport, which naturally was an open space, was meant to stay clean and cleared of debris. We all were responsible to sweep out the carport if we saw stray leaves, pine straw, or say a candy wrapper. To that end the carport held few items: our bicycles, Daddy's car, a covered metal garbage can and a toolbox.

Now this well-worn toolbox was special as it had been around for years and was moved from Waycross with tender care. It was the size of a small trunk, made of wood that had aged to a dark and shiny brown over the years, with a hinged clasp to keep it closed.

Being the size it was, the tools were limited to just the essentials: hammer, various screwdrivers, pliers, wrench, wire cutter, tire pump, oil cans and extra rags for cleaning up. There were other items, but I had no idea what they were. All I needed was the little squirt can of oil to use on my bike chain and the wheels of my trusty metal roller skates, plus the tire pump to add air to our bike tires.

One day after the completion of another of their many car projects, probably an oil change, they had cleaned up and put their tools away as Mother liked. We all were sitting at the table eating dinner in the kitchen that was just off the carport, when suddenly we smelled something burning.

First, we looked around the kitchen, and then we followed the trail of smoke to that very same old wooden tool chest. The moment Daddy pulled up the latch and opened the lid, a flame flared up quickly. Wow!

In his usual calm way Daddy grabbed a skillet to snuff out the fire. After a few attempts at getting the flames to die out, he had everything under control. He knew it was an oil fire so water would have made it flame more.

Mother had done just such an action many times on the gas stove, when the bacon grease in her iron skillet suddenly flared from spattering. She plopped the top on that skillet. Flames would be smothered, and she could continue her frying of whatever was fried that day. But let me continue about the non-food grease fire.

How had this wooden-box fire suddenly erupted? It seemed to be a mystery. Again, Daddy knew exactly what had happened. We had just witnessed the phenomenon known as spontaneous combustion.

Probably one of those oil rags had been sitting in the closed box with the sun and heat of the hot summer day bearing down on it. The oily rag must have started to smolder. When Daddy opened the lid, air hit the smoldering rag and the blaze had ignited. Another lesson learned.

My two brothers did not need any encouragement to keep their cars clean for each vehicle was a thing of pride and joy. Many hours of washing, scouring those wide white wall tires, and polishing every bit of paint and chrome on the outside and inside took time. They shone with pride.

All the men in the family seemed to react to situations in a level-headed manner. Well, most of the time anyway. Thinking back to that act of marvel with Tommy being rescued by his brother's quick and unselfish action, started me realizing just how strong family ties were.

As remarkable as that feat was alone, the strange thing was that the boys had surely been arguing about something or other before the entire hullabaloo started. They did that a lot.

Those brothers may have had times of disagreement but mostly they enjoyed doing things together. They could tell jokes only funny to them and laugh hysterically. I pouted because they had their own stuff going on that did not involve a little sister.

The duo of Kenny and Tommy made up a bond of close Brotherhood they shared always.

Kenny's '50 Ford with Judy, Beverly Booth,
Carole Kelley, Robert Howard and Don

CHAPTER TWENTY-NINE

Two Brothers, One Sister, Adventures

There were many fun times with Kenny and Tommy. If Kenny's friends were going swimming or somewhere exciting, I would pester him to take me along. He was usually good about this and even would let me bring a friend. He also had a paper route plus a job at the nearby Texaco Station at East Lake Center. He earned enough money to be able to buy his car and gas, allowing him more freedom. He was a hard worker and liked his independence.

Since the gas station was at the East Lake Center, I liked to walk up there to see my brother. There was lot to do at the Center for there was a drug store, a Colonial Grocery store, hardware store and best of all Wilson's Ice Cream Parlor where I loved to get a banana split!

Just across from the Texaco Station was the Scottish rite hospital for children on Hill Street. On some of my walks if the children were wheeled outside to get some sun, the nurses would allow me to talk with those sick children. Sometimes they even let me read stories to them, so I could share my favorite pastime and give them something to smile about at the same time. Those were special times.

If I went along with both my brothers for car rides, I could go a lot farther than my walking or biking. Sometimes we went to Snapfinger Creek where we would swim, slide on the rocks, and jump into the fast-moving water. Not far from there was the Misty Waters Park, where the older kids liked to swim and bring their friends to hang out and socialize. On the way home they sometimes even treated me to a Dairy Queen Chocolate Dipped Vanilla Cone. Life was good.

Kenny and Tommy's relationship was typical of brothers just two years apart in age. Sometimes they were buddies and other times they were bears, fighting bears.

They were notorious for their fights or brawls. Kenny would usually pounce on Tommy and before long they would be wrestling and yelling. They made headlocks, leg locks, arm locks, and so forth, but there never seemed to be any real punches landed. The aftermath was always a lot of huffing and puffing and scowls, but no black eyes or cut lips.

Yes, my brothers seemed to either be doing some project together, being pals, or they were at each other's throats. Sometimes literally, as some of their arguments turned into shoving or wrestling matches.

I hated these and remembered one of their tussles especially because they had started fighting in the living room of our home. Well, Mother would have none of that, so she got a pitcher of water.

"All right, Boys, you stop that right now or this water is going right on top of you." She held that pitcher of water over them. Miraculously, those two looked at each other, well, glared at each other, but stopped.

Neither one of them wanted to mess up the house, especially the living room, especially with Mother scowling down at them. Mama could give a look that could peel the paint off the wall. They knew she liked things, clean, neat, tidy, and shiny; yep, that rule and Mother's threat stopped that particular fight cold.

I always cried after their wrestling matches, naturally. I was accomplished at crying by then. My brothers picked on me without mercy, punching me in the arm or shoving me away. The deadly one-knuckle punches made my arms bruise. It was super great because I had black-and-blue evidence, they had really hurt me. I bruised very easily so it was an ongoing ploy that started losing its punch after a while.

No amount of whining, pouting, or holding my arms up as evidence ever made a bit of difference. It did absolutely no good. Ten minutes later they would be right back teasing me again, calling me the dreaded name of *Judy the Cootie*. Yet what can I say, I loved my big brothers and always wanted to be around them.

Yeah, I know that sounds really dumb, but as much as they pestered me, they also laughed with me, played games with me, and made me feel like a loved little sister. So, I took the good with the bad and loved them back.

Robert Howard and his sister Nancy were our neighbors and Kenny's friends who went with us at times to our various outings. Millard Lide also would join us, and I liked that because his sister Betty was my age, and we could hang out together away from all those teenagers. There were Glenwood Springs, Clifton Springs, and Lake Spivey. Most of the time I would just walk down to the McKoy Park Pool, my bathing suit rolled into my towel, rent a locker, then spend the day in the sun and water with my own girl and boy friends.

In the 1950s Stone Mountain was another place of interest mostly because of the unfinished carving on the side of the exposed granite mountain. There was not a big park, mostly picnic tables scattered here and there.

The only tourist place was a little wooden structure with a window. A lady would sit and sell picture postcards and little bags of granite and other rocks.

Sometimes our church would have a hayride and we would ride out to Stone Mountain. The ride alone was a lot of fun, naturally, after our arrival we would have a picnic. Then we would climb to the top and enjoy the spectacular far-reaching views of the Atlanta area. Since only about one third of the giant granite mountain is visible there is a lot of granite in Georgia and the Carolinas

The cool thing about spending the day around the mountain, was how pure and beautiful it was. We would go quite close to the base where the smaller rocks accumulated below the carving. You could look up to see the scaffolding on the side of the mountain where the workers were carving all the enormous figures. There were many trees for shade and even a rippling stream. We surely hoped this special mountain would stay just this way, a natural and beautiful place for us to enjoy.

The woods and dirt roads around the mountain were very popular places for young love birds to park. Tommy was on one of these little jaunts one evening with his girlfriend Jean, when his car got stuck in the dirt road. There were very few paved roads near the mountain, and they were way out in the middle of nowhere with no help or phone booth nearby. It took a lot of time for him to find someone who could help get his car unstuck. Tommy rarely was in trouble, but this time was a big exception

It was quite early in the morning when he tried to sneak into the house, looking muddy and forlorn. Daddy caught him, oops, Poor Tommy. Daddy also made him apologize to his girlfriend's father. Knowing my Daddy, I would imagine he tried not to break into a little smile when Tommy stammered his way through the explanation of why he was late. He was rarely if ever in trouble, but I doubted if that stopped him from future trips to that magical Stone Mountain.

We used to have many wonderful trips up to the Mountains and parks in North Georgia, Tennessee and North Carolina. Mother was born in Manchester, Tennessee so naturally one of our favorite adventures was seeing Lookout Mountain and Rock City. There were little red bird houses along the roads inviting you to "See Rock City," sometimes even painted on tin barn roofs.

A day's ride could lead us to mountain adventures. We enjoyed all of North Georgia's beauty.

CHAPTER THIRTY

Dogs Roving all Over

"Please, please, please, can we keep him, Mama?" I implored with my hands held prayerfully under my chin.

My mother had heard just such a plea before; maybe she will weaken this time. I continued my pitch to keep the pup, "He just wandered up while I was raking leaves in the back yard, and he looked sad and lonely. Isn't he cute?"

Mama looked down and seemed to see an animal totally different from the one I saw. She saw a scrawny, dirty, full of sand spurs, and rather mixed-breed, shaggy dog. She did, however, see his big, tearful brown eyes.

Seeing her weaken a little bit, I quickly added, "He just needs a bath and a little food, and I will comb out all those twigs and stuff and he will be beautiful. Plus, I will be sure to take care of him all by myself and feed him and all. Please?"

"Judy Reach, you are something else, every stray dog that happens to come into this yard seems to head straight for you."

"Yes ma'am, that's because they know I will love them, and I always do, don't I?" Since she did not use my full name this time, that meant she was not too mad.

"Well, yes, you do, I must admit." There was a pause as I held my breath. "Then what happens when the owner comes looking for him, or he runs away from here, or gets hurt?"

Boy Howdy, she was hitting all my weak points. "I know, I know, but I promise to be good and not cry as much this time if something like that happens."

Then I heard her soft words, "A few days, just a few though, just to see how he behaves."

After another long pause, she added slowly, "Grab some of those old towels and put them in the carport for him to lie on and I will fetch some leftovers and water."

As Mama continued with the stipulations, I breathed a giant sigh of relief.

"Remember, he is for you to care for, not me, not Daddy, not Kenny, not even Tommy, although I already know you will try to get Tommy involved with this particular stray. He looks like Butch, the dog he loved so much."

Now Joey joined the list of animals our family had while living on this corner of Spring Street. We had a revolving door of doggies as many of them passed our house on the way to who knows where. Since Adams dead ended at our house where McKoy Park started, it made our yard their last hope of a home, or at least a morsel of food.

There were very few fences in our neighborhood, creating a free range for animals to roam and rove at their will. It seemed mutts meandered here and there and everywhere. Whether feathered or furred, we loved our pets.

Our first pets in Decatur were Ike and Willy, the cute cocker pups we brought up from Waycross. The two dogs started getting bigger and more beautiful as they grew. Many of my parent's friends asked to buy them. Sadly, they decided to do just that because it had gotten very hard to keep the big dogs corralled in our yard. We were sad, but also glad both brothers went to one home to stay together.

Hortense was our only feathered friend, besides my blue parakeet. Percy stayed in my room where I could let him out to fly freely, but only in the bedroom. He escaped just once and flew into the living room, perching atop the drapes. Mother did not appreciate one bit the little gifts he left behind on those beautiful drapes. I loved that little blue parakeet because he was all mine.

In Waycross when I was about four, we had our one and only kitten. I would hold him and ride around the neighborhood on my trusty tricycle. Mother said she was allergic to cats and would gag as if cat hair had gotten into her throat from my itty-bitty kitty. He was never allowed inside, naturally. One day that sweet little white kitten just disappeared. I looked everywhere; he was nowhere. I cried, but everyone else seemed to be fine with his absence. They never got all the sweet cuddles and the purrs he gave me.

Daddy grew attached to one big Wire-Haired Terrier that visited us regularly. He named him HayWire, the perfect name for, again he was the expert in names. I found his fur too stiff and curly, but Daddy thought he was funny and fun. HayWire followed him around the yard and liked retrieving a thrown ball. Hortense was gone by then and Daddy liked having a new companion.

Tommy became attached to Butch, the biggest dog we had. He was a gentle and furry large Collie mix. The whole family got attached to that sweet dog. If you notice, I never mentioned their eating or sleeping in the house. Mother would not allow that at all. However, she always was the first one to add an extra blanket for them during cold spells. Butch loved to sleep in the big tent when my brothers would pitch it in the back yard.

I got quite attached to a Manchester Terrier that friends gave us. Buddy was a handsome little guy with a shiny black coat and was not very big. Buddy really liked to rove and roam our neighborhood, but he always came home. Tommy and Kenny also got attached to Buddy because he had a spunky and fun attitude. He did eventually run away and stayed away, sadly.

Then there was our little puppy we were given. He was not a stray, and we rarely had puppies. My room had a door to the back porch allowing me to sneak him in to cuddle and play. Eno was the name Daddy settled on quite cleverly. We were given the little white puppy with black spots on the Vernal Equinox, thus shortened to Eno. That little gangly sweet puppy got big fast, too big to slip into my room. He became a magnificent looking, loving, loyal dog and companion. He was my pal; Mama loved Eno.

There were other overnight visitors roving through our revolving door, but we could tell when they were just passing by for a handout. We gave them food and water and let them take a nap if they liked, then they would leave.

Rovers

Some doggies stayed only a day and then they just went away.

Some slept, drank, and then ate, thinking that was perfectly great.

Others stayed quite a while longer, our love for them was stronger.

Short or long their stay mattered less, giving a dog loving care was the best.

CHAPTER THIRTY-ONE

Rock 'n Roll and Fashion

"Hey Kenny and Tommy, Elvis Presley is on the Ed Sullivan Show," I called out to my brothers. "Quick, come and watch him and see if they will show his *swivel-hips* tonight," I sang out with excitement. My favorite singer was on TV, and I was not going to miss one minute of the show.

This is an essay I wrote about the 1950s music and fashion:

Yes, censorship had started, and we all wanted to see how Elvis did. Some people called him *Elvis the Pelvis*. My mother tsk-tsked at that unseemly term. It made me want to see him on Television even more

Mother did however make one exception. "Judy, let me know when or if he sings *Peace in the Valley* or *Amazing Grace*. That young man can surely sing those gospels beautifully," she called out to me. It made me smile, she liked him too.

On this night Ed Sullivan called Elvis a *nice young fellow*; now that was progress. They had only showed him above the waist when he sang the last time. That must have been some kind of a nut who decided to do that. Next time though they showed his full figure, swiveling hips and dance moves too. At least this was one singer Mother would listen to without shaking her head trying to keep up with all the current songs.

There were cultural changes and differences being seen throughout the nation, but at the same time our individual worlds continued fairly normally. This started me thinking about how people were the same in so many ways. Two of these similarities were with music and fashion. I realized that the way people dressed and the music they listened to made social statements also.

Teenagers were teenagers and they loved fads, no matter where they lived. North, South, East or West from the pre-teen bobbysoxers to the older teens we all read the magazines, listened to the radio and watched television. With shows like *Dick Clark's American Bandstand*, we saw what those teens wore, how they danced and the popular songs everyone liked to hear.

A new type of sound had emerged, Rock and Roll. From what had been mostly country music, the big band sound, or ballad singers, this new type of jive music had arrived. Emerging from the roots of country music came a fast-paced, toe-tapping sound, soon to become known as Rock 'n Roll.

Elvis Presley was the one who crossed these rigid lines of country, soul, and ballad music. He had put swing into twang, soul into blues, and Blue Suede Shoes into rock. Yep, he set hands to clapping and toes to tapping that had never tapped before.

A new term was also applied to some country music and that became Rock-a-Billy with singers such as Buddy Holly, Roy Orbison, and Johnny Cash. Groups like The Righteous Brothers, The Kingston Trio, Four Tops, and The Diamonds could show off their talents right in our own living room on television and radio.

The crooners remained strong such as Frank Sinatra, Dean Martin, Pat Boone and Bing Crosby. Now television was making a huge impact on our culture. We could watch these singers perform, not just hear them on our radios. Perry Como, Andy Williams, Dinah Shore, and Patti Page all had their own TV shows where they not only sang but also had guests to introduce new talent.

Some young teen-age singers began marking a name for themselves like Theresa Brewer and Wayne Newton who caught everyone's hearts. Ricky Nelson first sang on his family's show Ozzie and Harriet with his older brother Dave catching a few girls' hearts. But handsome Little Ricky Nelson soon became my personal heartthrob; yes, I would swoon just thinking of him.

The times would never be the same as this new rhythm and blues style of entertainment started making an impact on the music world, sometimes controversial, sometimes a little risqué, but always exciting. The new music was playing a huge part in how teenagers acted, danced and dressed.

Even the latest craze to hit the country impacted how we moved. Yep, the Hula-Hoop was a way to learn to swivel your hips just like Elvis. At least that is what we all tried to do. If you could twirl two or three at a time you could really get people's attention, so there was a lot of twisting going on those days with or without the Hula-Hoop.

At the same time, it was an age of sleek and bigger car styles, high fashion in architecture, décor, clothing and hair styles. The ladies wore hats, gloves, dresses, and fun jewelry. The gentlemen wore their Fedoras, suits and ties and had well-polished shoes.

All looked sharp with attention to details such as the seam of the ladies' silk stockings being straight and the high heels in perfect shape. The hats the gentlemen wore had to have the perfect crease when tapped with the side of their hands. Chop!

Such striking looks caught my attention at the age of eight and has been a source of my loving fashion and architecture. Those were good influences just as were the nation's love affair with cars with sleek models, new designs and new car smells. Mesmerizing.

On the subject of fashion, probably one of the most important clothing items to make its own statement was the skirt. The full skirts were fun because they would swirl and swish as we danced the Jitterbug, Cha-Cha, or Calypso. These skirts required wearing at least two or three crinolines underneath to have them flair out just perfectly. These petticoats were put into starch and hung over the clothesline until they became crispy and stiff. Oh yes, we suffered for fashion, especially on those hot Georgia days.

The circular Poodle Skirts made of felt were a novelty for a short time. Mother made me a red one and sewed a little curly poodle patch on the front. Straight skirts were worn a lot, not by pre-teens though; you see we really called them *tight skirts* as they looked best when worn snugly. Pre-teens had few curves to hug, unfortunately.

The various sweaters and tops paired with the different skirt types were carefully chosen. Straight or Tight skirts demanded sweaters topped with little neck scarves, pearls, or even fuzzy collars. Finish the look off with a wide stretchy belt and you looked *keen*. On our blouses we would wear scatter pins, usually a group of three little pins such as butterflies, flowers, and of course poodles. As you can see poodle dogs were the dogs of choice. I even had a Poodle Cut hairdo. I loved accessorizing with scarves, pins, and pearls

Then there was the subject of slacks. Girls were not allowed to wear slacks to school and surely not to church. When we did wear pants, they were any length you could want, from ankle to upper thigh. Long pants were tapered, even *pegged* if the legs had too much flair. This look required making a fold at the bottom of the pant legs and sewing the fold tightly; pegged pants were a little difficult to take on and off.

Then there were the mid-calf pedal pushers, even shorter Calypso pants, both worn tight. The guys wore Bermuda shorts, but girls usually wore the mid-thigh Jamaica's or even short shorts. These were fun and usually, worn with little slip-on flat shoes or ballerina shoes. Oxford lace ups, penny loafers and Keds could be worn with both slacks, and skirts. Popular with the guys were penny loafers, Bass shoes, or Oxfords always perfectly shined. Others wore high cut Black Converse Canvas shoes to look extra cool.

The choice of slacks fell into two categories, chinos or blue jeans. One fad involved khaki or navy Chinos that had a little buckle on the back. Supposedly if the guys wore them unhooked it meant they were not going steady with anyone at the time. I suspect that was foolishness though, but everyone did love to flirt.

Jeans were worn with wide cuffs and topped with striped tee shirts. The dressier slacks required button shirts, especially those made of madras or oxford cloth. This was a stylized decade where girls and guys spent a great deal of time looking just so; you wanted to look cool.

To finish off these looks the crowning glory of hair had to be just right also. To go along with that poodle skirt there was a short, very curly hairstyle called the *poodle cut*. Mother gave me a Tony home perm to achieve that style, and it looked quite cute. The short-bobbed look was popular. My sister also kept her hair short and pretty for work.

Now the girls with the long hair had more choices. They could wear a ponytail tied with a scarf, sassy pigtails, or have their hair down and loose. The longer-than-shoulder-length hair was usually worn in a tucked under *Page Boy*, very chic and lovely. The sleek pulled back *bun* or *French twist* looked very sophisticated. Colorful barrettes, head bands, and scarves were fun. *Bobby pins* and hair curlers were a girl's best friends. A little uncomfortable for sleeping, but no matter, it was for fashion after all.

The guys had their own hairstyles. One fashionable look was the *flat-top* or *crew cut* that required the use of Butch wax to keep the hair standing up just right. My brother Tommy liked to wear his hair this way. Others wore their hair slightly longer, with a part on one side. My brother Kenny was blessed with beautiful blond wavy hair, so he wore his hair however it came out when he combed it that day. It always looked perfect.

Then there were the *greasers* who wore their long hair swept back into *duck tails* on the sides, this required they always carry a comb to keep the hair always in place. You could see them using one hand to comb back their duck tails, while following behind with their other hand to smooth them perfectly. The comb went into the back pocket of their jeans, and then they would look to see how many girls swooned after watching that little grooming technique.

This group usually wore blue jeans with white tee shirts so they could roll their cigarette packs if needed into the sleeve. Those jeans always fit nicely, let me tell you.

You can see the various styles worn were indicative of what group you belonged to such as the perky cheerleaders, the smart group, the nice kids, or the *fast* group. The girls in this last group would wear very tight skirts, tight sweaters, and lots of make-up and some even smoked cigarettes behind the gym with the *fast* boys. Well, I never, and yes, I mean I never did that, no, not nice Judy Reach!

Culture was being thrust upon me from all sides. I was learning that to be *cultured* meant learning manners, appreciating music, dancing formal steps, and having social graces. There were also separate cultures in the world, each with its own set of values and standards. The world was changing for sure, and this was just the tip of the iceberg for what I needed to learn in the years to come.

There was one thing for sure, Rock n Roll and Fashion were here to stay.

Roy Reach, Grandmother Lily Wolfe Ashley,
Aunt Helen Wolfe Lanier, Judy, and Libby Reach 1954

CHAPTER THIRTY-TWO

Company is Coming

"Company's coming." That cheerful call rang out from the hallway that held the precious telephone. We knew Mother had been talking to someone at great length for her, about five minutes. She did not like to talk on the phone unless it was to her best friend Thelma Davis. Those conversations had lasted much longer.

"That was My brother Eric calling," she told us with a big smile on her face. We all loved Uncle Eric and his wife Aunt Barbara. They had two sons Ricky and Bobby; a few years younger than I was. All four would be here in two weeks for a three-day visit. Let the Company preparations begin.

My first thought, "*Neato, Uncle Eric and Aunt Barbara are coming. They are super!*" My second thought, "*Uh-oh, that means the cot for me.*" My final thought was, "*Oh yes, there will be two kids younger than me. I won't be the youngest one in the house, this is gonna' be terrific.*"

Mother and Daddy enjoyed having family come see us so it should be fun getting ready. Oh yes, *Getting Ready for Company* was a time-honored tradition in Southern households. For instance, the first time Uncle Eric brought his beautiful bride to meet our family, Mother had gone into one of her Lizzie's Tizzies.

Barbara was from Massachusetts and had a flourishing career as a Fashion Illustrator in Boston. Mother was faced with meeting her youngest brother's new bride for the first time right here in our home. The pressure was on, it seemed.

"Roy, she must be very sophisticated and probably is a very smart dresser," Mama made this statement in a way that spoke volumes. "Oh Dear, what will she think about us? I better put out our best china, silver, and finery to impress her."

Then she finished her never-ending sentences, "Oh no, I won't have time to make a new dress. I better see what I can wear."

"Now Libby, just settle down a bit and think about how she might feel." Daddy was speaking in his very understanding smooth voice, softly and slowly. Better be calming the stormy waters that were coming. He knew that storm had begun the minute Mama learned about this new *Sophisticated Lady* coming to town.

He persevered, "Think about it, Libby, she will be meeting her new husband's older sister for the first time. Why, I would say she is the one who will be nervous." Boy Howdy, my Daddy could sweet talk my Mama. Sure enough, she smiled and leaned in for a hug. She loved his hugs.

Now this upcoming visit was different because Barbara had been wonderful, and she fit right in with our family. Yes, she was a beautiful, very petite and very well-dressed lady who loved my mother's younger brother. That made her almost perfect. This visit would be more relaxed.

And so, the silver was polished, the crystal was shined, and the cooking began. Yes, the Company Dinners had to be planned. Cakes and pies could be made ahead of time. I loved helping with these elaborate preparations. The shopping had to be last minute to have fresh meats and vegetables. Our Frigidaire was not large and had a freezer compartment that was only as big as a half-gallon of ice cream, not much room.

I pitched in by making a batch of my chocolate fudge with pecans, and some fruit and nut cookies that had become my own specialty. Patsy had helped teach me a lot of new recipes for all sorts of goodies. Company Cooking was in full throttle.

Mama left an order for the next delivery from the Milk Man for extra milk, some buttermilk and butter. The bread man would deliver extra bread and even some little donuts and a coffee cake. Such treats were rare in the Reach household. See, having company coming was great for many reasons. This company visit would be a happy successful family gathering and it surely was.

Now all of Daddy's Reach brothers lived in Alabama. We visited them frequently and they became some of my most favorite trips. Their wives cooked everything Daddy liked, such as yummy fried fruit pies and chicken 'n dumplings.

His only sister Etta had married and moved to Ohio, and frequently visited us. Aunt Etta was very fancy with her fur coats and beautiful jewelry. There was one rare time when all four brothers traveled together to visit Daddy. He was the only brother who had moved away from the Alabama hills. Seeing those Reach brothers all together was a memorable time for Daddy. We had always driven up and down hills, into town, and into the farmlands to visit each brother and family. Having them in our home all together made me very happy. Daddy grinned as he told his stories, reminisced about those years growing up in their large family, and sharing the good and the hard times. It was heart-warming for they were all fine men. I did miss their wives though, but we would see our aunts soon enough on one of our trips to their homes in Alabama.

One of my other favorite visitors, well not truly a visitor because she was family, was my grandmother, Mama's Mother. Oh, how I loved Granny Ashley. She lived in Melbourne, Florida where we went on many trips to visit. Pawpaw owned a fruit packing business and gift store there. Sadly, he had died before we moved from Waycross of a Stroke. That meant Granny was living alone since then, so the family would have her stay with them for a period of time.

Uncle Billy, Aunt Muriel and Mother mostly alternated her visits as they were in Florida and Georgia. It made me happy when she was with us because she stayed in my bedroom with me. She took great care of herself, her grooming, and her health. I loved to watch her comb and brush out her long silky grey hair. She then made one long plait that hung over her shoulder. During the daytime she always wore her hair in a loose bun on the top of her head.

Granny was also quite a reader and even wrote poetry, which she put in her little notebook in her elegant cursive handwriting. She was one of my favorite people who I loved spending time with, just talking and listening to her poetry. She loved plants and birds and would show me pictures in the book she kept. She would write down and tell details of spotting a bird or an unusual flower. Sometimes if she met an interesting person, the details would be written in her floral language. My elegant Granny Ashley was a Poem herself in my eyes.

Mother's sister Muriel came down from Buffalo, New York now and then. While she and Foster lived there, they had three sons, Bedford (Buddy), Ben, David and daughter Suzi. On this visit there was only Suzi with them which pleased me to no end. She was my closest cousin in the family and just a couple of years younger than me. Suzi had long blond hair and an ever-present smile and we were more than cousins, we were friends.

In addition to the extra milk and bread deliveries, Mama flagged down the vegetable man. He was our favorite because he had a horse drawn buggy piled with fresh vegetables and sometimes fruit. Mother looked everything over picking just the right ears of corn, snap beans, green peas and perhaps a melon or some squash and tomatoes. While Mother picked and looked, I just patted the horse, he was sweet. That family visit was about perfect. Not only did I enjoy having my fun cousin to talk to, but she was also relegated to a cot like me, it was just fine.

Patsy and Tommy were living in their new home in Toney Valley, but they joined us for our Company and Sunday dinners. Tommy was always thoughtful to bring some surprise and Patsy would bring her delicious desserts. Kenny was now 18, Tommy was 16 and both were busy with school, jobs, cars, and dating, but they made a point to stay home for a change for those yummy Company Dinners.

Mother had only one sister and five brothers, the oldest being Admiral James Ashley. He was a naval officer who led his own ship in World War II. He was our handsome hero though we rarely were able to see him as he lived in California. Uncle George was another officer we loved to see. Colonel George Ashley flew airplanes during World War II while in the Air Force and was a world traveler full of charm, stories, and generosity.

He loved mother and as he traveled, he would look for treasures to bring us. We had a dainty China tea set, a Sake set, even an intricately designed Kimono. He bought us jewelry, fancy fans, even a tasseled Fez. Not only did he bring gifts, but he also gave us the heavenly air conditioner for our living and dining room. A cool retreat for us in those hot muggy summer days.

The next brother was the very handsome Bill who worked for Eastern Airlines. His pretty wife Jeanne was a stewardess with Eastern and Uncle Bill had been a supervisor. They had two children, Caran and David, my cousins. We liked to visit them in their modern split-level home in Miami. Uncle Billy had a smooth soft way of talking and was always a dapper dresser. I loved that whole family.

Uncle Eric was the youngest living brother who, as I have said, we were fortunate enough to have visited often. There was one more son of PawPaw and Granny Ashley, Sam, the last son and youngest child. Sam was a charming, popular, and good looking eighteen-year-old in Melbourne, Florida.

A terrible accident happened when he was riding on his high school float as King of the Parade. Tragically he was killed in that accident. It was a sad blow for the whole Ashley family. I never even got to meet him as it had all happened before I was born.

Well, let me tell you about the most volatile combination of family visits. If the Ashley Brothers, Uncles George, Eric, Bill and sister Aunt Muriel visited when their mother, my Granny Ashley, was visiting it seemed to spark high emotions. A lot of the tension at times could be between Granny and Mama. But if they lingered too long at the dining room table, trouble could arise.

Their calm family conversations, could escalate into a riot of talking, being overly emotional, and bringing up past sins and glories. Frankly, I never knew any details and understood even less. I just knew I loved them all and did not want any of them to be upset.

Listening at the door, I could not understand the muffled conversations one bit. They all loved one another so I knew they were not being mean. But between my mother's low stress level and Granny disliking any controversy, there had been only one way to end the situation. Granny would put the back of her hand on her forehead, flutter her eyes, sink back in her chair and faint.

Silence would fall over the group of siblings. Even Mama's mild-mannered sister, our Aunt Muriel was shaking her head over all the ruckus and swooning.

Next, we heard Mama coming, so we all moved back from the door. That swinging door could take some hard hits. I think steam was coming off the top of her head and her face was too red. "Patsy, take these three for a car ride. Maybe go to the Dairy Queen," she said distractedly.

We all said nothing but were smiling inside, so we did as she asked. We piled into the car and had a fun ice cream trip. I never minded those emotional visits, because I associated the loud visits with chocolate dipped ice cream cones. Was that wrong of me? Probably.

Evidently Granny loved the attention with all the fanning of her face, the patting of her hands and the water being given to her. That one act of *Swooning* caused all her children to pull together to help her. I did say my Granny Ashley was very bright with a flair for the dramatic. She knew what she was doing.

Company Coming was always fun for all of us, even Mama, after the preparations were done.

Our uncle Colonel George Ashley flew his wartime airplane into Waycross 1946

Emmet, Roy (Daddy), Clyde, Lloyd and Luther the Reach Brothers

Southern Food Menus in the '50s

• Fried chicken, scalloped potatoes, gravy, snapped beans
Biscuits, Banana pudding

• Meat loaf, mashed Potatoes, gravy, corn, pickled beets,
Biscuits, peach churned ice cream

• Tuna casserole, corn on the cob, pineapple cheese salad,
fried Cornbread, pecan pie

• Fried catfish, Brunswick Stew, Cole slaw, Hushpuppies,
pineapple upside down cake

• Fried pork chops, Potato pancakes, yellow squash,
deviled pea salad, Jell-O with fruit

• Pot Roast with Potatoes, carrots, onions, gravy, fried okra,
dinner rolls, Chess Pie

• Macaroni & cheese, stewed tomatoes, pears & cheese on lettuce,
Rice pudding

• Baked Ham, red eye gravy, sweet potatoes, green bean casserole,
Biscuits, Blackberry pie

• Grilled cheese or BLT sandwich, tomato soup,
Chocolate pudding and Whipped cream

• Chicken and dumplings, pickled cucumbers, onion and tomato,
Fruit tart

• Chicken & rice casserole, tomato and lettuce salad
Biscuits, Peach cobbler

• Fish sticks, tartar sauce, Cole slaw, creamed corn,
hushpuppies, Angel food cake/ berries

• Spaghetti with Meatballs and sauce, chopped green salad,
Garlic bread, Strawberry shortcake

• Chili with Grits and cheese, Saltine Crackers,
Jell-O mold with pineapples

• Hamburgers or Hot Dogs on toasted Buns, Potato Salad, pork and beans, Custard pie

• Chicken fried steak, Baked potato, creamed corn, Ford hook Lima beans, rolls, apple pie

Breakfast-for-supper meal:

Waffles or pancakes, eggs, Grits, toast with jam or buttermilk Biscuits, sausage gravy

New-Years-Eve-Good-Luck meal:

Hoppin' John rice and black-eyed peas, collard greens, 'pot likker', with ham hocks, cake

Stuff I would not eat

Pickled Pigs Feet • Pickled whole Eggs • Chitlins, Chitterlings, Pigs knuckles, Souse, and too many pig parts cooked in too many ways for me to mention!

CHAPTER THIRTY-THREE

T-birds, Trips, and Travels

As for my own travels, I did get to take a few trips. Uncle Eric and Aunt Barbara visited again with Ricky who was five and Bobby who was three when I was fourteen. They asked Mother if I could spend a couple of weeks with them. Me, just me going with them to Winter Haven, Florida, it must be heaven.

Another wonderful fact about this trip was that we would be riding in that fine and fancy new T-Bird Uncle Eric had just purchased. 1958 was the first year the Ford Thunderbird was made larger, and the style was greatly modified from the 1957 model I had always admired. This car had plenty of room for all five of us. It was fast, sleek, and a thing of beauty in my eyes.

Winter Haven was very green and lush, with many varieties of citrus trees, tropical plants and flowers everywhere. Quite a change from North Georgia. We went to the Bok Singing Tower and Cypress Gardens where the ladies wore long flowing hooped gowns, holding frilly parasols. Oh yes, also the Gardens were spectacular. I was in heaven.

I baby sat for Ricky and Bobby now and then and that was always fun because they were cool little guys. It was fun to watch them grow taller and older with each visit to our home. I had started babysitting quite a bit for neighborhood children and knew how to be a pretty good babysitter, for young kids and babies.

Uncle Eric also let me drive that T-Bird a little. They lived on a cul-de-sac, so I spent a lot of time going up, down and then around. Two more years and I would be joining the driving-by- myself-world like my brothers and sister. I was getting a learner's license soon and could then drive with an adult.

Uncle Eric had a twinkle of humor in his eyes and a smile on his face. He always called me Judy-Pie and I adored that name when he said it. Uncle Eric and Aunt Barbara were pretty cool in my eyes. I loved Ricky and Bobby, so being around them and helping with them was fun.

Aunt Barbara was quite an artist as she had been a Fashion Illustrator in Massachusetts, so she tried to teach me how to oil paint. I say tried because I just did not seem to have the knack; she was masterful with any art. I painted a blue vase that had a hanging flowers design on it. Well, my painting was of a blue vase all right, but the hanging flowers looked like monkeys suspended from a vine. Perhaps this lack of hand coordination had to do with my wandering and irregular handwriting. My whole visit with them was super, monkeys not mentioned.

Now the very first trip I took just by myself was when I visited Beverly Booth in Covington, Georgia. Beverly and I became pretty good friends after Patsy and Tommy's wedding. Tommy's sister Louise was married to John Booth, and they had three children, Beverly, Sally and Lamar. Well, this was a big deal because Beverly was having her Twelfth birthday party with both girls and boys. Since I had just done that a few months ago myself, I was eager to visit that terrific family and enjoy the party.

Getting to Covington was the first part of this Summertime adventure. They decided I could take a Greyhound Bus by myself since it was not a long trip. All by myself, mind you. I was excited and a bit nervous as bus trips were new to me. Mama made sure I sat next to a well-dressed lady who said it would be fine and she would watch out for me. She did and was a very nice lady. I never once worried about anything bad happening because my friends and I had taken the trolley to Rich's downtown many times.

It was great fun visiting with this whole family; they were warm, inviting, and Mrs. Booth was a great cook. Beverly's party was neat-o. The kids were dressed in their nice Church clothes and were friendly to me right away. Beverly looked pretty as always. We played games like pin-the-tail-on-the-donkey which was funny and kind of goofy.

Then we played a game new to me where we sat in a circle on the floor. A bottle was placed in the middle, and someone first spun it, evidently whoever it landed on had to be IT, but what was IT in this game? So, they spun once more, and it would land on a girl or boy depending on who was chosen first. *Wait a minute, wait one minute, what's going on here?*

Lots of snickering and giggles were going around the circle, the circle where I knew only one person, Beverly. Well, the spinning bottle landed on a girl, and they all went, ooohed, uh-oh, and strange snorts. What the heck? There was a boy already chosen, so I watched as the two went into a closet in the room. I was clueless as to what was going on with that closet game.

When the two of them finally stepped out, the girls face was red, and the boy had a weird smile. Bingo, now I got it, a kissing game. *Oh No, a kissing game.* No, I had never been kissed by a boy, well George pecked me on the cheek a couple of times, and I almost turned my head, and it might have landed on my lips. Ever since Mother told me the overly graphic Pandora Box story about Nature, I had avoided any such accidental Lip Kisses.

I decided to go along with the game now that I knew the rules, I was already twelve and should be able to handle it, right? Right. Well, that devil bottle spun and spun and finally did land on me and then on a boy that was kinda' cute. We slowly walked into the Dark Closet, not knowing each other at all. Silence, feet shuffling, throat clearing, and suddenly I felt lips on my cheek. I was out of that closet lickity split, red faced, and safe. But the party was a lot of fun.

When we went swimming in the Covington pool one day, all was going well, and we were having a super time. Swimming and diving were really my favorite summer pastimes. Beverly and I decided to go diving, which we did very well a few times. I looked over at their high diving board and it seemed to be about the same height as McKoy pool's. I climbed the stairs, hey why are there so many steps? *How high was this diving board?*

I warily walked to the end of the board ready to show off my diving skills. As I looked down into that glistening blue water, my stomach flip flopped. Now what? No way would I climb down, so I gathered my best gumption and dove. Oh, I was losing control of my so-called-show-off dive and hit the water wrong. A shooting pain soared down my legs, I was helpless in the water.

I may have blacked out for a little time, because someone had pulled me out of the pool and laid me on a towel. *Oh no, it was that cute lifeguard*, wait I am dying of excruciating pain, and I am embarrassed? Beverly, Sally and Lamar were worried, I was worried, my whole body was worrying.

Beverly's Mom was there somehow, and I was being helped. Mrs. Louise Booth was wonderful and cared for me so sweetly. The doctor said I had sprained my back when my legs flipped over too far, ouch, no more high dives he said. That was one of my best trips with Beverly and I had to go and sprain my back. They were all thoughtful and caring and my embarrassment finally went away. I had to be retrieved by my parents, so my first independent bus ride was only one way.

That trip was still wonderful, I made new friends, had fun and just had one big *oops* on my part. Thank you, Booth family.

My new favorite trips were to see Patsy in her newly built home in Camilla, Georgia. Yes, they moved far away from Decatur. Tommy Cullens had purchased well over one hundred acres of pecan groves in Camilla, his hometown in Southwest Georgia. This was a whole new territory for me and a different life for Patsy. She loved it and was very proud of their new red-brick home with the white-columned front porch with white rocking chairs. Their home grandly sat behind rows of pecan trees and was wonderful in every way.

They even had some cows and Hampshire hogs. It was all amazing and new to me. We had always lived in towns with no acreage or farms close to us. I was in some kind of heaven when I was able to visit with them, just me. It was fun to ride in their truck around their property to check out everything. I even watched them shake the trees to let the pecans fall all around. We would sit in those rocking chairs to crack and shell the nuts, hopefully in halves, not broken. It was fun, different and kind of exciting.

We went shopping in town, visited Tommy's home and family, and went to their Methodist Church. This town was just the right place where they would build their own family. Their firstborn was a son, Tom, who was born on the first day of September in 1958. I loved that little baby boy and was a proud aunt to my sweet, feisty, pretty sister's first child.

Taking trips with the family or by myself was always an adventure with more places to explore.

Eric and Barbara Ashley, Mother, Granny Ashley, Judy, with Ricky and Bobby Ashley

CHAPTER THIRTY-FOUR

Faith-Filled Structures

"Uh-oh," I think to myself. "Daddy is pacing." With my bedroom being right next to the kitchen I could hear Daddy rattling his ever-present pocketknife, lucky sea bean, and coins in the pockets of his suit trousers. Daddy expected punctuality, which meant he looked at his watch a lot while waiting. He knew exactly how long it took to get to any destination and his internal timetable was always at work to keep us where we should be, and on time. When we heard his coin-rattling nervous habit, it was the signal that we needed to move.

"Are you about ready for church yet?" Daddy called out in an impatient voice that meant, hurry. "I am going to wait in the car for all of you," He finally conceded.

Now where is that other shoe clip for my new little low-heeled shoes? There it is.
I looked in the mirror proud to see the beautiful baby blue dotted-Swiss dress mother had made for me. The knee-length dress had a full skirt shown off by layers of stiff crinolines. Mother had accented the bodice with four rows of grosgrain ribbon. I like that touch because it showed off the beginnings of a figure and my changing shape. At that point anything helped my self-esteem as it was up, down, and all over the place. Thirteen was hard, fun being a new teenager, but still it had its trials.

My brothers had always liked to tease me, but now their teasing would cause my tears to flow. Then in the next minute I would be giggling at something they would say. Gee, is this what my sister and mother were trying to tell me about hormones?

Enough on that subject for now, let's get back to the Sunday morning schedule. We were all packed into the car and finally heading to our destination, the Fifth Avenue First Baptist Church. You would think we would have had this ritual trip down pat, as we left every Sunday at 9:30 for Sunday school at 9:45, then Church service at 11:00 and usually returned home by 12:30.

Then on many Sunday nights we would go to Training Union and evening service, which I really liked. We had more social activities, which gave us time to talk with our friends and plan some functions or outings for the Teenagers. The evening church service also was more casual with a lot of singing and music.

There were times though that I did not want to go to church. Perhaps if someone had hurt my feelings, or I was upset with another person, who knows why, but those Sundays I just did not want to be in church. Mother could tell when I was quite sick or just being difficult, but most times she understood and would let me stay home. I mean Kenny and Tommy were always going on dates, or out late Saturday night, and Sundays they too did not want to attend church. But you know most of the time we did go, even if it was grudgingly and we did have a better day, but I never admitted it to Mother or Daddy.

Our Reach family always seemed to sit on the left side of the church, lined up in the pew a few rows from the front. The sun would shine through the stained-glass windows bringing a warm glow into the church. It was always nice to see our family all looking neat and well dressed. Daddy in his grey suit and Mother in her navy-blue lace edged dress, Kenny, and Tommy all spiffy in jackets and slacks, and I was enjoying seeing it all. Everyone had their Bible in their hands ready to follow the sermon.

When I was eight or nine sometimes it was hard to see if a lady in front of me had on a fancy hat. Now if she wore a fur stole my eyes would bulge in fright when I saw there was a beady-eyed animal biting his own furry tail. It was hard to concentrate, and I was glad Mama did not have one of those creatures around her neck. However, she did often wear grand hats, some with veils, but never tail biting fur things.

Reverend Russell Case was our Pastor. He was not a big man, but a mighty presence he was indeed. He would preach of sin or sorrow and how we all needed to be saved to be able to walk the heavenly streets of gold. His sermons were always interesting, deep, sometimes humorous, but always teaching and preaching the love and word of God.

In the next minute he might stop, slow down and ask us to bow our heads and sing *Just as I am* or *Amazing Grace*. He was a sincere and faith-filled Pastor who truly lived what he preached. Our church was a bit conservative, not making too much noise during services but occasionally, a soft *Amen* could be heard or a sniffle now then, or maybe a laugh at a funny story he would tell us. Mostly, you would see people following along with their ever-present Bible, listening to the teachings, and singing hymns with joy together.

His wife was not only beautiful, but also quite talented with musical instruments. She played the organ masterfully on Sunday mornings, but for the evening service she played the grand piano. I loved to sit on the front right pew to watch her play the piano. She really could get everyone singing as she played those hymns.

George Mitchell smiling in the middle of his friends.

I was in the middle giggling or making others giggle.

Another instrument she would sometimes play was the xylophone. Now when she played that along with Brother Case trumpeting on his trumpet, the rafters of that church would seem to rattle, especially if you were seated in the balcony. Music and singing were a big part of our church. At the Sunday night services we sometimes watched movies of Billy Graham's preaching. He was a wonderful and dynamic man. Yes, there was more than singing and organ music, we were taught Bible lessons and life lessons. In fact, our mother was a Sunday School teacher and played the piano for the classes.

I listened to it all and learned a great deal, but also listened with my heart. It was during this time when I had just turned thirteen that I had a strong inspiration during the service. As I listened to the words and thought of all the Sunday School lessons and teachings, suddenly everything became perfectly clear. It was as if looking through a clear pane of glass rather than a foggy one. I understood the words deeply at that moment. During the benediction, I quietly slid out of my pew and walked up to the front of the church where the pastor smiled and took my hands in his.

A few weeks later I was baptized, an emotional and moving event for me. I wore an all-white dress, while waiting expectantly to go up the steps. As I stepped into the Baptismal pool of clear blue water, Reverend Case's warm smile made me feel assured. He took my hand reassuringly. Yes, this was right where I should be right at that moment. As he lowered me back into the water I was overcome with a feeling of peace and calm as I came up from the cool water. It was strange and wonderful at the same time. I knew this was the right choice for me to make because I felt a sense of calm never experienced before that time.

Since I was now a teenager, I was able to join the Girl's Auxiliary or GA's. This was a group of teen girls learning Bible verses, and many good lessons in Christianity, and along the way having a good time with my friends. There was even a Coronation ceremony upon our completion of the studies. It made us feel like debutantes as we wore evening gowns and were presented with Certificates. Some of my school friends were part of this group, Susan Huff, as well as the twins Janyce and Joyce McClung. Linda Moss was another one of my church and school friends.

From that time, I began taking more seriously the teachings of the Bible. My parents had instilled in me how to act and treat people as you would like to be treated. Mother stressed to me that the word hate should never be used. She knew there would be times I may dislike someone but try to never have hatred in my heart. Treating people as I would like to be treated always worked well.

Daddy instilled in me that honesty should always be a priority in my life, especially when dealing with others. But it was also important to protect myself from danger or harm by being alert and observant. One thing Daddy did not like was dishonesty. Since his work was in seeing that laws were respected and kept, not misused, or abused, that is how he lived his daily life

Mother and Daddy had certainly tried to instill in all of us the values of a Christian life of honesty, virtue and good behavior, but it was mighty hard for us to always follow these rules.

I would try harder to be better, yes, I would. The new sense of peace helped calm my emotions.

Fifth Avenue First Baptist Church entire Sunday School class 1953,

GA Coronation

CHAPTER THIRTY-FIVE

Keeping up with Stuff

Oh, the joy of living on a hill overlooking a street overlooking a park and wide open for everyone's observation!

As I walked up from the park on a busy Saturday morning, I saw waving on our clothesline, four white, what looked like half-moon stiff flags, waving back and forth in the breeze. Next to these were three of my brassieres, four pair of underpants and one nightgown.

"Oh No, Oh Geeze, look at that, it's my stuff flapping out in the open for the whole world to see," I groaned out loud.

My eyes blurred and could not see if there were any other of my things dangling for the public's inspection.

I spun around to see how much of the whole world was looking. Hmm, not too many at that moment so I said a quiet *Thank You* for that, then climbed up the bank. Quickly running to the clothesline, I yanked down the most embarrassing items. The clothespins flipped here and there. At that moment, I did not care about the flipping clothespins.

Now that I was fourteen, I had learned not to get too upset over stuff. Wait a minute, that did not sound right even as I thought it. Well, I was trying not to get upset, but every month my emotions would go crazy, and I couldn't seem to control myself. Yes, I was trying. It just did not work well all the time.

So, I said in a nice calm and only slightly quivering voice, "Mama where are you?"

Then came a muffled voice, "I'm in the bedroom mending clothes."

It sounded as though she had pins in her mouth. I didn't like it when she talked with pins in her mouth. One day she would inhale, and they would go straight down her throat. I worried about my mother. She did a lot of dangerous work around the house just to take care of us.

There she was sitting at her sewing machine working on our clothes for loose or lost buttons, rips, stains, or any other problem that needed fixing. Doing stuff for us, not for herself.

Back to my very dire situation. I held up the evidence I was about to quietly discuss, "Its Saturday and these were on the clothesline," I stated bluntly, "Out there in the open."

These words came out as though a crime had been committed. I knew better than to talk to Mama like that. I sucked in a deep breath.

"Well, Miss Judy, Saturday is the only day I can starch your crinolines and wash your underwear so you will have them for Monday. But I do usually try to hide them better."

"And you are supposed to help me starch those petticoats you know, it's a messy job," she replied this in one long breathless sentence in a tone I knew very well.

She really was good at turning things around. I felt bad, she was right.

"Yes, Ma'am, I'll go out and get the rest of the laundry.

First, I retrieved the errant clothespins that had flipped here and there. They didn't deserve such treatment, after all it wasn't their fault, they were holding up my underwear out here in the open.

I laughed out loud when I took down the stiff crinolines. They were fun to flip around, but I had to fold them in half and place them in the clothes basket.

The rest of the clothes were easy as I gave each item a good shake then smoothed them, folded them and carefully placed each piece in the clothes basket. A little careful folding and smoothing cut down ironing time. Since I had to iron sometimes, I knew all about that.

As I continued to slide the clothespin bag along the line and drop in the wooden clips, I started thinking then saying out loud, "This is all my stuff. None of this belongs to the boys or Mama and Daddy. I guess I should help a little more with my own stuff. I will try harder."

Maintaining clothes was important. We couldn't just toss out a shirt if the buttons were missing.

If there was a rip in the knees of the blue jeans, they had to be saved. When clothing was purchased, they were intended to last for a long time, at least until we grew out of them. Then they were passed down or given to someone we knew. I was the last in line but with two older brothers, hand-me-downs were slim pickings.

Mama was in the middle of a weekly chore while doing the wash. This is when she checked each item of clothing before putting it into the wash. If there was a repair needed, she set it aside to fix before she washed the item. Her repair sewing basket was always nearby for quick fixes. She was a whiz at ironing on patches for torn jeans or repairing rips and tears. You could hardly tell where a mishap had taken place when the item was returned.

We all, well with the help of our mother, maintained and retained our own stuff as I said.

However, Daddy taught us how to keep up with our shoes. For this task he had a well-worn wooden shoe-shine box that had been around for as long as the wooden toolbox in the carport.

Hey, Daddy must have built both of those well-worn boxes now that I thought about it. Anyway, the shoeshine box had one handle with two bins on each side. One held the tins of shoe polish, one each of black, brown, and tan with three soft rags and corresponding color stains on them.

The other bin held two brushes used to buff each shoe to a high shine after the polish was applied in little circles.

"Make 'em shine like a baby's behind," followed by Mama saying, "Roy!" Those were the words I remember.

Oh, and there was one more addition to that dark brown box, a bottle of liquid white shoe polish with a sponge applicator. This was used on the Oxford shoes and on my white canvas tennis shoes. To clean these required scrubbing the red clay spots out first then drying well. Then I dabbed the white polish carefully on the canvas so it would not soak in, oh how they gleamed.

We all had our own stuff to keep up with and we were not supposed to bother anyone else's stuff. I learned that the hard way when I was younger and was not going to go through that learning process again. The consequences of those learned lessons were painful.

Just as I said, I was fourteen now and could handle everything in a calm way, well at least my own stuff, well, most of the time.

Judy at 9 helping Mama hang up 'drawers'

CHAPTER THIRTY-SIX

A Day on Decatur Square

Could there be any more fun than spending an entire day with a good friend window shopping? I think not, and Shay and I hoped to enjoy walking around the Decatur Square and poking into the stores just off the Square. We began our exploring just before the Square a little past the Decatur Movie near City Hall.

Shay and I laughed thinking about all the fun times we spent at the **Decatur Movies**, especially when there was a double feature. In the summer it was the coolest place to be with their air conditioning

First, we had to buy our movie treats like popcorn, an all-day Charm cherry lollipop, Milk Duds or Coke and life was perfect for the next three or four hours. *Oh, yes.*

Following the World News Reel, Previews of coming attractions were played. That would get us all excited about coming back again to see those new movies. Many funny Cartoons were shown, Bugs Bunny being my favorite then Tom and Jerry, Mickey and Minnie Mouse or Woody Woodpecker.

Many times, on Saturday they ran serial shows like Buck Rogers, Captain Marvel, Superman, and maybe Mr. Wizard. I loved all the science fiction movies, but enjoyed any movie they played, just to be able to hear and see everything bigger, brighter, and louder than on our home television .

There would be an Intermission before the second feature film that allowed for live entertainment on the stage in front of the screen. There might be acts like the talented Yo-Yo Man, a Magician, or even a Cowboy doing rope and lariat tricks. They were all fun making us laugh, clap, or squeal out loud.

Shay and I had both shopped at the **Belk Gallants** Store recently shopping for school clothes, so we headed to the next stop at **Clark's Music store.** That was always a blast because there were glassed-in listening booths to spin some 45-platters to try out the tunes before we purchased anything. That was rarely. But I could listen to the Righteous Brothers sing *Dream, Dream, Dream,* over and over, swooning the whole time. Shay had her favorite songs to hear so it was fun for both of us.

There was always a broad selection of sheet music that I liked to browse through. I decided that day to buy Mama some sheet music by Glen Miller. She would be happy to have his music to play.

Miller's Book Store was a treat to be able to poke around the new bright books. Going into the bookstore to smell new books and flip through the interesting titles was always fun. However, my favorite place to look for any book to read or get any information was our school library. Looking through the card catalogue you could retrieve any book you needed in the stacks. The Dewy Decimal System kept the books in their proper order.

Not just books were at the library, but tables to read or study. That quiet place was like a retreat from the hustle and bustle of the halls and classrooms. However, there was usually very little time for me to use the library for studying. Maybe that would change in the next few years.

Shay and I decided a little food might be a good idea since we were just passing **Jacob's Drugstore.** We smiled thinking of all the good stuff there was to eat at that counter. We had to be careful with our money, so we shared an order of hot crispy fries, and each had a cherry Coke. We felt like resting longer on those red spinning stools but decided to continue our journey on the Square. We knew **Lane's Drugstore and McConnell's Five and Dime** were not far away with delicious pineapple sodas with vanilla ice cream, or maybe a thick strawberry milk shake.

Being teenage girls, we liked to look and try on clothes in the various **Dress Shops**. That day there were several beautiful hats in one window, so we went in to try on some of them. We felt special in that elegant shop trying on this or that hat while sitting at the dressing tables. Shay and I looked at each other and giggled.

What fun it was to look cute, sassy, or even just a little sophisticated that day.

Sorry Ma'am, we were just trying, no buying today, maybe next. time.

We continued our walk passing the **Men's Store** and the **Haberdashery.** Daddy had bought hats there.

There were several **Banks** and a few **Business Offices,** but we skipped those. I did always look forward to the times Daddy let me go inside one of those banks with the impressive lobby.

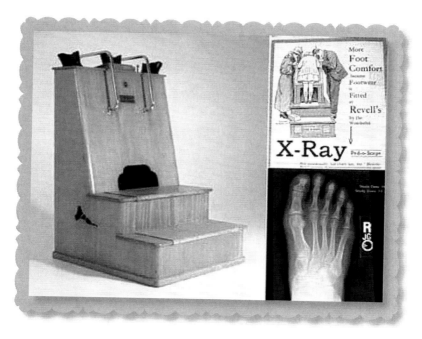

Thompson Bolan Lee Shoes was just around the corner with their strange *X-ray booth.* You would slip your foot in and look down to see your bones to tell how the shoe fit your foot. It was creepy. I preferred Mother's nice **Ladies Shoes Store** across the street. I don't need to see my bones to know if I want a particular shoe, thank you very much.

The very large, very beautiful **Candler Hotel** was just ahead. We decided to wait until we could bring our Mothers with us to enjoy the **Tea Room** inside. Oh, they served delicious pastries and goodies just like the

Magnolia Tea Room at Richs. There was also a wonderful **Cake Box** nearby that also had yummy cream puffs.

The Derby House was next, where Tommy picked up the Atlanta Journal newspapers for his paper route delivery. If I ever went along to help, he had me wait in his car out of sight. There was an unwritten teenager boy rule that bringing little sisters inside was not cool. Okay, I just helped fold them.

Shay and I almost went inside to get a hamburger, but decided we were getting sort of tired.

Finally, we walked up the granite steps into the North entrance of the **Decatur Court House,** the heart of the Square and the heart of Decatur. Inside there was a quiet atmosphere where we felt we should whisper.

We looked up at the tall ceilings and all around, then went into the museum room, full of memorabilia and precious items. We were different from many teens because we enjoyed Museums. We exited through the South doors, down the steps and wound up not far from where we had started our walk that morning Shay and I had shared a terrific Day on the Square together as best friends. We both loved Decatur and that made this little Day on the Square not just enjoyable, but very special for both of us. Plus, we did buy a few treasures.

North view of Courthouse

South view of Courthouse

CHAPTER THIRTY-SEVEN

Hi to High School

That long awaited day had finally arrived, I was going to Decatur High School. It seemed like forever that I had been waiting to be a teenager then to be old enough to go to High School. Also, I would be going to the same school as my brother again. This time though, instead of being the big seventh grade older class in school, I would be starting on the lowest rung of the school ladder.

The eighth graders at High School were called Sub-Freshmen. Could there be a worse name for a class than Sub-Freshmen? The only thing that made it halfway easy to take was that we were at last, High School Students. Yes, 1957 had finally arrived. I planned to say Hello, Hi! Yes, I Am Tommy Reach's little sister. My Name is Judy, not Jodie, J-u-d-y!

Well, here it was one of the most important days in any young girl's life, and I was staring into my closet with a look of blank dismay. "Mama, what can I wear today?" I pleaded.

"What are you talking about, for Heaven's Sake?" Mama said in what I considered a very exasperated voice. "All we have done for a month is concentrate on your clothes, your shoes, your hair, your underwear…" she trailed off.

"Please, don't talk so loud about you-know-what. I know, I know, you are right, maybe I am just nervous," I admitted.

"Now look, this plaid straight skirt with the blouse you found at Belk Gallants is cute. I think it looks just like what we saw the girls wearing at the open house we went to a few weeks ago. I was taking special note of what they were wearing so we could find you the right clothes."

She spoke this in such a calm and logical way that it all sounded perfectly right.

"Thank you." She shook her head, smiled, and went to the kitchen. Mama knew I would be fine.

The school clothes shopping day was a few weeks ago at Belk Gallants. It had been such fun knowing we were going to buy something, not just look. And we were not buying any embarrassing undergarments.

I had noticed there was a big shoe sale that day and had to go try some on while Mama was looking at scarves. All the shoes were wonderful, especially the leather ones. My eyes landed on a pair of Capezio flats that looked perfect, black slightly-pointed-toed flats with little straps. I asked for my size hurriedly as I knew this could be pushing the limit.

The lady found a pair and I sat down to quickly slip on the shoes. I stood, took a few steps and the shoes felt like heaven. Quickly putting them back in the box, I asked the sales lady if I could show them to my mother right over there. She hesitated, but who could say no to that pleading face?

She nodded. Then she watched the exchange as I begged Mother, who shook her head. I pointed over to the sale sign, the sales lady weakly put her hand up to the half off sign with a small smile. The two of us walked over to her and Mother said, "My daughter tells me that these are very well-made shoes, and this is a good sale. Is that true?"

"Why, yes Ma'am Capezio is a good brand of shoes made of fine leather. And they are quite stylish right now. They looked pretty on your daughter," she added in a sales pitch voice.

"Well, that would complete her outfit nicely. I think we will take this pair. Can I pay for these other things here, please?"

My face may have stretched a little with my big smile. Mother was being extra nice.

Now here it was today, and I was slipping on those very same shoes. This was going to be a good day and at last I was prepared for my higher education.

Tommy was already calling for me to get into the car. I finished brushing my hair and putting on a little lipstick before grabbing my purse, notebook, and books. Those textbooks had been ready for days. We had carefully covered each one in the brown paper grocery bags. They looked sharp with just the school subject on the front of each book. Neat.

Yes, I have mentioned that I like school, but this was High School, Cheese 'n Crackers!

Tommy was always so cool. There he was in his very clean and very shiny Plymouth looking just as neat and shiny himself. His Butch haircut was standing up straight and his plaid shirt was ironed crisp and tucked into his jeans. My brother always looked sharp. I am sure his jeans were cuffed, and his loafers shined to a gleam.

Tommy held the back car door open to let me quickly jumped into the back seat. That was much more difficult than usual as I tried to balance the books and bags. He first picked up his friend Chuck who lived just down the street. He hopped into the front passenger seat looking spiffier than usual.

We turned down McKoy Street to Shay's house where she was already waiting at the end of their driveway. She looked prettier than usual in her sharp new outfit from Casual Corner. Her brown hair was turned under perfectly showing off her smile. My best friend Shay was always looking very pretty.

Tommy turned to the back seat and said, "See, Judy, that is the way to be ready to go every morning." He and Chuck shared a big guy chuckle, they thought they were funny.

Shay smiled and we giggled, who cares we were on our way. And in the blink of our wide eyes, we arrived at Decatur High School.

Oh Gee, here we are, Oh No, here we are, I thought I said this to myself.

Looking over at Shay, I could see she was looking at the school. Three huge buildings loomed before us. We were going to walk ourselves to death going between all these buildings. We looked at each other, neither of us moving. *What do we do now?* The guys were out of the car already, but then Tommy came back.

Center Building, Gymnasium and Auditorium

"Hey, you two, I gotta' lock up the car. You need to go over there to the North Building," He pointed toward that far away building, then urged. "You don't want to be late on your first day," he said giving us a sly smile.

Oh, didn't he know so much? Yes, I had to admit to myself, he probably did.

"The North Building way over there? Why did you park so far away? It looks like it is a mile away," I groaned as I started to walk.

"Right in the middle, *right in the middle*," he smugly said pointing with both hands toward the Main Building in the middle.

Shay and I began to walk too slowly and then picked up speed as we saw other guys practically running toward the building. Yeah, they must all be Sub-Freshmen. Well, we were too but we wanted to look a little bit cool. We did however fast walk to our Homeroom class.

Our very first High School classroom would be Homeroom, every day. This is where roll call would be taken. I wondered if we would all be together in other grades. As I looked around there were very few kids I knew, even Shay was not in my Homeroom class. No, but there were a few from Fifth Avenue Elementary kids there, thank goodness.

Our Homeroom teacher was Mrs. McGeachy who had just begun her first teaching assignment at Decatur High. She seemed younger than the other teachers and I liked her right away. Her eyes were very watery, and she explained that she had just gotten Contact Lens.

Now I was not sure what they were, but they were glasses that fit right onto your eyeballs. Yikes! That sounded awful and she kept blowing her nose and wiping her eyes with a handkerchief. She had a funny sense of humor; we all liked her. It was going to be a fun year ahead. She also said she wanted to give us some parties. Parties, imagine that.

Having located my locker at the open house, I knew where it was. Today though I wanted to carry my books for a while, just to be sure, even though they were heavy. I had the little card for my schedule of classes that I thought I had memorized all the class numbers. Then when the bell rang, students started pouring out of rooms like ants from an ant hill, I froze.

Oh No! Where do I go? Whoosh, Swoosh, they blew past me. I turned a few times in panic, then a familiar face appeared. I felt my face redden.

"Hey Judy, glad to see you!" said my friend Blake McCloud. "Where ya' headed?"

"Oh, just headed to Algebra," I croaked, casually twirling my hair coyly, so tightly that my finger got stuck. *Get hold of yourself, Judy, try to act cool and calm.*

"Hey, me too! C'mon, we can go together," he said picking up his pace and clearing a path through the ants, ah, students that is. Holy Cow, how did that happen? However, it did, I was glad that it did.

Homeroom was done and now I was seated in Algebra, check. Blake was in this class, good. Hope Shay is all right. We have American History together.

There was a man standing by the blackboard, my first man teacher. He was trying to tell us to start writing down some strange math problems. They were diagrams, maybe I will like this math after all I liked English diagrams of sentences. Kenny and Tommy had this subject, then Geometry and higher Algebra.

As I continued to muse in my own shallow thoughts about my hair or whatever, I heard a stern deep voice saying, "You, young lady, do you know the answer to this equation?" He was staring right at me.

Who, What, Where am I, What did I do? I blushed so deeply my toenails much have turned red along with my face. I snapped out of my trance enough to say quietly, "No sir, I don't know the answer."

There it was, the first day of High School and I was already a failure. Mortification struck me speechless on the first day. Maybe I should have glanced through those books instead of making sure the covers looked pretty. Quickly I was realized a big fact of life, *High School was not third grade*. I better shape up quickly or I will be floundering in the hall being run over by teachers and big ants.

South Building in the snow

Oh, I also forgot about my plan to say hello to people. You don't have time to think around here.

Where was my mirror? Did I still have on any lipstick? Was my hair messed up from all that running, hair twirling and bumping around? Help!

And so, it went that day. An endless running from class to class, building to building, passing through the gymnasium on the way to the south building. This is where I said *Hello, Hi, how are ya', Whatcha' Doin'? and Hey!* to people passing. I smiled, nodded, and flirted and flipped my hair and just greeted others all day. There were many new faces and cute boys, really cute.

No, I didn't know people but after a while it didn't matter, some people said Hi back and next time they would remember me, maybe. Well, let me say I was tired, my feet hurt, I had trouble finding some classrooms, and I was not sure where to go at lunchtime and so forth but all in all it was a wonderful first day.

The rest of the day I paid close attention to each teacher and did meet up with many of my friends from Fifth Avenue and that was fun. Shay and I ate lunch with some old friends, and some newly made friends. We ate the cafeteria food that day, but I ate too quickly to know exactly what we ate. My smile had returned, and I was even able to crack a few jokes, until it was time for gym.

Gym class, now what in the world was someone thinking when they imagined any girl would want to wear this ridiculous blue one-piece short outfit? Especially in front of anyone to do anything much less do it in public. This was going to be a long year of gym classes.

Oh yes, and one final little sister note. Two people asked me if I was Tommy Reach's sister, not Little, but Sister. I do not know how they knew, but I beamed and said, "Why yes, I am. My name is Judy Reach, thanks." they waved and kept moving.

The first day of school was all that I imagined except for the more than few things here and there that needed to be fixed, in addition to my attention problem. I needed to work out a bathroom schedule in relation to my stops at the drinking fountain. That was learned after I had to run quickly to find the bathroom.

I liked Decatur High School, even being an eighth grade-Sub-Freshman with a lot to learn. On that first day Tommy had made sure that Shay and I were gathered up and delivered home. As he dropped each of us off, I felt as though we were being dropped off like deliveries of the afternoon newspaper, drop and go. He quickly took off for unknown regions that only Seniors knew.

Decatur High School North Building

Today that was fine because my body was aching, my feet hurt, and my head was swimming. I just wanted to think about this neat day and tell Mama about it.

Back and forth from building to building for classes

Fashions of the '50s

Lady's Wear:
School

No slacks allowed! • Shirt-Waist Dresses • Straight or Slim Skirts Button-up Sweaters •Blouses and Pullover Sweaters • Full, Circle or Poodle skirts with Crinolines • Sheath dresses • Boat or Sailor Neck Blouses • Cinch Elastic Belts • Fuzzy collars • Neck Scarves • Beads Scatter Pins • Heads Scarves for windy days • Oxford white socks Capezio flats • Slip Ons

Casual Day

Slim legged slacks • Capri Pants • Bermuda Shorts • Pedal Pushers • Short Shorts • Pullover Tops • Tie at the Waist Blouses • Sleeveless Blouses Skirts and Dresses • Strappy Sandals • Slip on Flats • Deck Shoes • Tennis Shoes Loafers • Oxfords

Office

Conservative Dresses below the Knees • Skirted Suits • Shirt Waist or Sheath Dress • Straight Skirts • Blouses or Sweaters • Sweater Sets • High or Low-Heeled Pumps • Seamed Nylon or • Silk Hosiery • Garter Belts or Girdles • Usually no slacks at work for the ladies

Church or Wedding

Higher Heels • Gloves • Hats with Nets • Sheath, shaped Dresses Pearls or Necklace • Clip Earrings • Slacks were frowned upon at most churches.

Evening or Formal

The Little Black Dress • Skirts to the Floor or Waltz Length • Full Skirted dresses to the floor with Hoops or Crinolines for fullness Choker necklace • earrings • High Heels

Men's Wear:
School

Chinos slacks creased • Navy slacks • Levi's Blue Jeans • Madras plaid shirts tucked in • Cotton or linen • Long or short sleeved shirts • V-neck sweater Pull-over shirts • Penny Loafers • Oxfords • Basketball canvas shoes, Converse The 'Smokers' had their own style, jeans cuffed, tee shirts, mostly white, sometimes with a pack of cigarettes rolled up in the tee sleeve and ducktail haircuts with the sides slicked back

Casual Daytime

Khaki pants • Bermuda shorts • Pullover shirt • Sweaters • Poplin Button down collar shirts

Church

Sports jacket • Cordovans • Linen button up shirts • Light Weight suit Shirt and tie • Trousers with belts • Black or brown laced shoes • long sleeved shirts

Formal

Suits • Tux • Black lace up shoes • White shirts • Black suit • black tie Cuff links • Tie pins • Tie bars • Watch fob

CHAPTER THIRTY-EIGHT

Circles Join Circles of Friends

As the days at Decatur High became routine, I discovered there was more free time to spend meeting my classmates. This was my goal. Tommy told me often to meet as many people as I could and remember names. Well, that was hard, but he said to say their name three times. Yeah, try that while running down the hall meeting someone else. I truly did try.

The plan to meet new people was working. It seemed the combination of the classes I was taking plus the friends I had already made at lunch, was providing me with a good base for some great friends. I had my old friends from Fifth Avenue and my new friends had become their new friends too. My circle of friends was growing, and we were becoming a group of fun guys and gals. We laughed and joked, were kind of smart and funny, were not mean or stuck up, and we were nice to people. Yes, we each had different talents, and some seemed to be leaders.

At Decatur High School the meeting place for kids was in front of the center building, the auditorium and gym. Mostly people liked to sit along the long rock wall to hang out and talk and meet. So that became the gathering place for people to enjoy in between or after classes. There were a lot of students who gathered in those areas.

You could tell the students who were involved with sports when they entered the gathering areas. Some I knew from Tommy playing basketball and tennis. But the football players were the easiest to spot, they looked taller, stronger more than most guys, and walked with the confidence they deserved. Who would bother these guys anyway? I was a lowly 8th grader, but I still could admire those older students, especially those wearing the cool Sports Letter Jackets.

Of course, I already knew a lot of Tommy's friends who were already Seniors and would speak to them. That caused an outbreak of questions like, "Hey, do you know him? or, "Tell me his name over there, that tall-handsome guy, or just tell us about any of them."

The obvious answer from me was, "Well yeah, he's my brother's friend." In a way I became a bit of a star for a short time, but I was not sure if it was the right kind of star I wanted to be. The final inevitable question was the very biggest unanswered one, "Will you introduce me to him?" *Oh geeze, no.*

Tommy had also warned me about the kids to stay away from. He said you could usually tell by the way they dressed, like some of the girls wore too much makeup and bright lipstick. They wore tight sweaters and skirts; then he said they sashayed their hips around guys and hang out with the tough guys.

Wait just a minute, what was he talking about? Well, I did not have girls like that in my classes, did I? Then I began looking out for those girls with tight skirts and sweaters, wearing bright lipstick and swaying their hips. They were everywhere I looked. Then I caught a glance of myself in a mirror and realized, I *was one of those girls!* Maybe not too tightly skirted, but otherwise I fit right in with everyone. Perhaps it wasn't the same though since my curves were not so curvy.

The tough guys wore their hair slicked back on the sides in duck tails, it looked kind of cool to me. Wait some guys had a cigarette behind their ears. Look at those guys over there, they have on jeans like Tommy. Oh, wait a minute, they were pretty tight and then they turned around, and oh, they were *really* tight. I better stop watching. *I could not stop watching.* What was wrong with me, was I good or bad? Maybe a bit of both. That seemed okay to me. I would make up my own mind in my own way.

Most of those guys were wearing white tee shirts or short sleeved shirts with the sleeves rolled up. A few had packs of cigarettes rolled into their sleeves. Oh yeah, they had on those black tennis shoes that laced up real high. Gosh it all looked so different than I was used to seeing, and I had to say, not too bad to me.

As I watched them, some of those guys and girls headed to the back of the building. What was so interesting back there, I wondered? "Oh, look smoke is coming from the football field. Something is on fire," I said as I tugged on someone's arm and pointed.

He laughed, "Yeah, that's just the smokers. They aren't supposed to smoke at school, so they go to the back of the school building. They get away with it for a while. Nobody wants to mess with them."

"Why not," I innocently asked. He was a sophomore, so he should know everything.

"Well, they are pretty tough to handle sometimes," he replied

"This is the first time I have seen them, but they look nice enough to me."

He snorted, "Well, yeah, maybe some are. Some have tattoos, ride motorcycles, and hang out with rough people. Not all of them. I don't know, I keep away."

Hmm, thinking to myself, I only saw five or six and I wouldn't want to stay away from all of them. I must talk to Tommy about this. This is something I need to think hard about.

After working out all these different ideas and opinions, I made my own choices. My ideal idea was to do high school my own way, the way that made sense to me and made me the happiest.

By the end of the eighth grade our circle of friends had grown from Shay, me, and our Fifth Avenue friends, to Martina, Jackie, Neal, Warren, Freddy, Gail, Johnny, Ann B., Pat, Johnny Mac, Judy T., Adele 'Posse', Jeanne, Billie Gae, Barbara, Jean, Janet, Reba, Allan, Sandi, Patsy, Susan,

Martha, and David, with many more to come. Whew, lots of neat people, and making more friends every day.

As my circles of friends joined circles of other friends, my life expanded there at High School.

Freddy, Martina, Judy, and Warren after school

The school was rebuilt and changed several years later after 1959

CHAPTER THIRTY-NINE

Twirling and Whirling

As the eighth grade was ending someone mentioned to me that they were holding tryouts for the Twirlette Squad soon. How cool it would be to make that squad. They were Freshmen and Sophomore auxiliary twirlers to the Majorettes, who were Junior and Senior students. Those Majorettes were talented, pretty, and sharp in their nifty uniforms. I had to try out for Twirlettes.

There was one small problem, I had never twirled and had no baton. My friends Jeanne Bellville and Martina Gifford decided that was no problem. We would find teachers to teach us over the summer. We did just that.

When I finally had my baton in my hands, it was love at first sight. It was very shiny with a white top and tip. I immediately tried to twirl it but all I could do was make silly circles. Yep, I needed those lessons quickly if I hoped to twirl well enough to make the squad. I was quite determined.

Barbara Holt was one of the head majorities and was one of Tommy's friends. She gladly agreed to give lessons at her home. I was in awe of this gorgeous Senior who could twirl, toss, catch and even use fire batons. She was a terrific choice to teach us almost-Freshmen girls.

We were eager to learn as we practiced repeatedly. Barbara taught us twirling moves, dance movements and routines along with marching until gradually we gained confidence. We were able to do more than just hold on to the baton, we could catch those shiny batons we had tossed up in the air. Miraculous.

We also discovered there were sore muscles in places we never knew even had muscles. Oh, the Charlie Horses we had, the aching arms and legs, and blisters on our feet, but all worth it. We finally were getting pretty good with our marching in unison and doing the routines perfectly. What a joyous achievement that was.

Barbara's house was near our friend Adelia 'Posse' Cochran, so on some days we hobbled over to see her and rest our sore muscles before our walk home. Barbara Archer was our friend who would often be there to join everyone. Posse's house was like ours where kids felt comfortable coming to hang out for a while.

It was getting late in the summer, and we knew our lessons would soon be over, sadly. Barbara was proud of us and said we were ready for the Try Outs that were coming up soon. She was a sweet, patient and talented person who we adored and appreciated. She prepared us well, even though there were differences in the way each of us had finished. I knew I needed more practice, but I would twirl my heart out to be better.

The day came when Barbara told us we had learned enough to be Twirlettes and one day even be Majorettes. She gave us certificates of accomplishment for learning so well. She also made us realize that if we did make it, there would be many days of practicing with the group at school. There would even be a Baton Camp. Our eyes sparkled with happiness mixed with sadness to have to end these lessons, but our goal was to be Twirlettes. We hugged her and said we would do our very best to make her proud of us.

The day finally arrived for the Try Outs at Decatur High. There were a lot of girls, too many I was thinking, as I stood with my baton in my shaky hand. Some of the girls had learned more quickly than I had or could do the leaps higher than I could, even do the routines better, but I was determined to try out anyway.

With a great set of nerves, I stood before those judges. Evidently, I stood still too long doing nothing until they said, "Judy, you can begin now."

"Oh, it's my turn. Oh, I'm sorry, I think I am a little nervous." They smiled with what I hoped was understanding and waved me to start my routine. I then managed a smile myself and began, doing pretty good but not perfect. High School was making me realize it was a lot different from elementary school where I sailed through some things. The seas were much rougher here.

When the list was posted all our group made it, although two of us were alternates. That was all right with me, I was still on the squad. As it turned out, they decided to make both of us alternates as regulars. Life was getting good, and those uniforms were very cool, even though the skirts were really short, almost like flared short shorts, blue and lined with gold satin. And the hats were tall with plumes and fun to wear as were the white boots, topped off with big tassels that we learned to make ourselves out of navy yarn. The one word for our uniform was *Sharp*.

My summer was still filled with days at McKoy Park, going to Saturday Movies, and skating with friends. But Twirlette practice was first. Shay began walking with me to practice which made it more fun. Well, with encouragement, determination, and the will to succeed, I became much better.

My muscles were sore no longer and the Charlie Horses only came with too much high strutting like we would do in the parades around Decatur Square. I really liked marching in formation, so sticking with the practices became an important part of that summer of 1958.

But there was nothing like the first night when we marched and twirled at the halftime during the Decatur High Bulldogs game. We had a super football team, so it was with pride that we did our routine on the field. We had practiced with the band and the majorettes and knew our steps, but it was still making me a bit jittery to face this first game. When the band started playing, we began marching out in unison. Then being under those bright lights on the field, all nervousness suddenly faded away. This was just going to be fun, and it was.

Nina Gae Miller was next to me, Jeanne, and Martina nearby. We all beamed because we knew we could do this; we did do quite well. I looked up briefly at the announcer's stand where Tommy would always have been giving his play by play of the game. I think he would be incredibly happy to see me twirling and marching at this half time of the Decatur Bulldog's game. By the way, Decatur won that game.

One of our dance routines was to the popular song *Tequila* by *The Champs* that had a Calypso beat. It was such fun for us to perform that it became a favorite.

All of us were excited after our first game and decided to go to the canteen to play the juke box, play pool, or dance to the music. There were always a lot of guys who joined us. Life was looking pretty good sharing the time with everyone. Oh yeah!

The bus rides to the away game were a lot of fun. It took several buses to transport the Band, Twirlettes, Majorettes and Cheerleaders and the gear that went along with each person. I only left my uniform on the bus one time and Coach Hall made sure it got back to me before the next game. He was a terrific coach.

The games we played in North Georgia were a lot rougher due to the very cold weather, sometimes even snow. Those short uniform skirts did not provide anything to make us warm, so we wore sweaters under our jackets, and flesh-colored stockings that helped. What helped the most were the flaming *smudge pots* they would sometimes keep along the sidelines, otherwise it was brrrrr. We hurried back to the stands to get our coats, mittens and earmuffs!

In the Springtime we marched around the Square in a Military parade and a Boy Scout parade to name a couple. Depending on the length of the parade, we might have blisters and sore legs, but no matter, marching and strutting were great fun for all of us. We always had our boots polished sparkling white and would make new navy tassels for those boots to strut and twirl proudly for our Decatur High School.

As the year went on, Football season was ending, and Basketball would be beginning soon. Well, the Senior Majorettes felt some changes needed to be made. They thought there were too many baton twirlers on the field at football game and there probably were. They wanted just our squad to try twirling at the basketball games, wearing white socks and sneakers instead of boots on the gym floor. We didn't want to make a big fuss about the whole situation, we just liked to twirl.

We did just that and had fun. We sat with the Cheerleaders, did our little routines at the break and everyone enjoyed the show. Yet we could feel the winds of change blowing in and feared this could be the end of the Twirlette Squad at Decatur High. Talk was going around about a drill team or a flag team, or some such squad. Next year there going to be big changes, at least different from twirling batons.

Twirling and Whirling was fun, but with changes, where would that leave us?

TWIRLETTES: *Left to right, first row:* J. E. Henderson, J.Tucker. *Second row:* M. Gifford, P. Hale, L. Webb, B. Sams, E. Suddeth. *Third row:* D. Short, J. Bellville, S. DeLoach, G. Miller, J. Reach.

Twirlette Squad 1957-1958

3rd row: Diane Short, Jeanne Bellville, S. DeLoach, Nina Gae Miller, Judy Reach

2nd row: Martina Gifford, Phoebe Hale, Linda Webb, Betty Sams, Elaine Suddath

Front: Head Twirlettes: Jo Ellen Henderson and Janna Tucker

Our Twirling Teacher Barbara Holt, a Head Majorette in 1958

CHAPTER FORTY

Tommy Takes on the World

Tommy had been preparing himself since elementary school for entering a college or university after graduating from High School. Looming too quickly ahead was the time for him to make some decisions. Hopefully then he could be awarded some good scholarships for he wanted to pay his own way, or that is what he told me. It was all confusing to me and four years away.

It seemed to me he really was preparing himself for a successful future. I knew he was going to be leaving home soon. It was a sad realization. But I was proud of Tommy for making excellent grades and doing well in sports. He was a good guy working hard to pay for his car, gas and spending money. He also realized, now that since he was dating, more money was required.

Tommy was attending classes on how to give speeches with the *Toastmasters* and how to be successful, even how to run a small business. He had set goals for himself and to achieve those he had joined the R.O.T.C where he had become an officer. He was also a class officer, on the student council, on the *Indecatur* staff and a Senior Superlative.

His accomplishments were impressive, he was even on both the tennis and basketball teams. Tommy also had joined the Junior Achievement program to learn how to build a product and sell it as a small business. One of those projects was building shadow boxes. He had a natural talent for the modern business methods taught in the program, and it came as no surprise when his projects were highly successful. Oh yes, and Mother loved his two beautifully made shadow boxes for our Living Room wall.

Since Tommy wanted to present himself to the world in a positive way, he took the Dale Carnegie courses to be able to Win Friends and Influence People. He was a Senior *preparing for the world*, as he liked to say. I was only preparing for the ninth grade.

Being his little sister, I was immensely proud to have him as my older brother, but I thought, Geeze I have a lot of stuff to do in the next four years. Would or could I ever achieve even half of what my big brother had done? There I was at fourteen just trying to figure out what to wear to school the next day and remember to finish my homework. It was a lot to live up to following the path of Tommy Reach at Decatur High School.

His steady girlfriend was Jean Haynie. I thought she was the most beautiful girl I had ever seen. Tommy and Jean had become one of the popular couples at school, even being Superlatives together. Jean came over to share supper with us sometimes when we could see for ourselves how happy they were together. Jean worked at a radio station in Atlanta, sometimes even singing beautifully on air.

She let me have a little project of my own to help her, *Neat-o.* All I had to do was hurry home after school to watch Dick Clark's American Bandstand and write down the top ten songs that day. She rewarded me with a stack of 45-records. By keeping up with the latest hits, not only did I get super songs, but it helped the radio station. Watching all those cool teens dancing and listening to the music, was fun.

Tommy's hard work, dedication, and diligence paid off as he neared the end of his senior year. With the support of Senator Richard Russell of Georgia, he won a coveted appointment to West Point. It was the United States Military Academy located on the Hudson River in New York State.

We were all very proud of him. He had also applied to and been accepted into the more recently formed Air Force Academy. That Academy had been established only four years prior in Colorado. Man, oh man, he had two acceptances, two offers to consider.

Tommy thought long and hard on this difficult decision between two such good academies. Since he had been a member of the ROTC at Decatur, even becoming an officer, he decided he liked the infantry better than flying at that stage of his life. So, West Point it was for my fortunate brother, but now what would our life be like without him around? The Reach family would miss his gentle humor, kindness, and wit, with a little of his mischievous nature now and then.

There was that one special job Tommy had shared with me that showed his patience and kindness towards me. Any time spent with my brothers was a good time, but this one was super special to me. I have mentioned this before, so here are the details according to my view.

"Tommy, please, please, let me go with you tomorrow on your paper route," I implored my older brother. He had his own wheels now since he was sixteen and had graduated from his trusty bike for delivering newspapers. He bought a 1949 gray Plymouth, not the prettiest set of wheels on the road, but he loved it.

Tommy's paper route was across town off Clairemont Avenue, new territory to me. Naturally this roused my curiosity and sense of adventure. What I did not realize was that his job meant getting up, dressed and out the door by before 4:00 AM. What? Wait a minute I might have to change my mind about this whole thing.

After what I thought was way too much thinking about his answer, he finally replied, "Well, OK if you promise to do as I tell you. When we get to the Derby House to meet the other carriers and pick up my packs of the Atlanta Journal newspapers, you must stay in the car."

He said this like it was really a big deal or something. I never understood why my brother didn't want his little sister tagging along to meet his buddies, but I did as he said.

When Tommy returned from his oh-so-secret meeting, he had a huge stack of newspapers. My eyes bugged out looking at that stack, now what do we do? What we did was fold them just so and tuck them in tightly to make nice, neat little packages of papers. Yes, he allowed me to help with that.

How had my big brother managed to look perfect, even before there was a hint of light in the sky? His hair was just right, his jeans and shirt looked great, and he acted all chipper. Looking down at my own outfit, I realized my shirt was buttoned wrong, my socks didn't match, and my hair was not combed. It did not matter as long as I was right there right then.

I didn't tell Tommy, but I liked doing all of that paper-folding project with him. After completing our folding task, we headed to the location of his route and then things began to look better. By then it was about five in the morning and to me seemed a truly magical time of the day, even before birds began their daily chirping. Everywhere we went in the Clairemont area the streets were quiet, the houses were dark, and the calm stillness and beauty of the morning was amazing.

Tommy would give me about ten newspapers with strict instructions as to where to place them, not throw them, but carefully deliver them to each house or apartment. I only messed up a few times. The quiet beauty of the morning that we were sharing was no longer work, but fun.

Being with my brother, who I adored, and sharing the gentleness of this quiet time was a joy. Walking those neighborhoods on his paper route, and seeing the lawns covered with morning dew sparkling from the rays of the rising sun creeping higher in the sky, was truly a magical experience.

A lot of his route were apartments, but I had never actually been inside an apartment building. My first encounter was a three-story apartment. When I opened the door on the first building I was greeted with stacks upon stacks of stairs. It was actually only two sets of stairs, but lots of climbing with the many buildings. The good thing was that you could do apartments much more quickly than the spread-out neighborhood homes.

I was learning. In fact, I got to really like apartments and thought maybe I would even live in one someday. Tommy let me go with him other times after that and I gradually got every paper delivered correctly.

The summer of 1958 was difficult for me knowing I was losing my big brother, when he would head to West Point. That also meant I would be the only Reach child left at home. Tommy had graduated from Decatur High in a wonderful ceremony and since then he had been busy packing for his trip to New York. I was very proud and happy for my brother, but immensely sad at losing my pal. He was the one I went to if I ever needed to talk over a problem.

Mother and Daddy had been bursting with pride for their son to be going to the U. S. Military Academy. He had worked hard for it and surely earned his spot at West Point. But when the day came when he was leaving, there were many tears on the way to the airport for his flight.

My Daddy kept wiping his eyes, but Mother was sobbing, and I was hugging him. He saved me for last to say goodbye, but the emotions had been so strong it was all I could do to try and make a joke like we always did. I told him I would send my chocolate fudge and cookies to him. He promised to write letters just to me besides the ones to Mama and Daddy. The tears flowed. Tommy left.

Tommy was about to begin a brand-new life and future; I was simply worried about being lonesome.

Morning

Shimmering sparkles from the sun on the dew

Reflect to the world a bright new dawn.

The morning light casts a rosy hue

That spreads warmth across the lawn.

High in a tree a small bird sings

And tells all it's time to rise.

So, the solitude of morning wings

Into a bright new day of pale blue skies.

Judy Reach

2-4-63

Tommy Reach and Jean Haynie Superlatives

Tommy Reach, Decatur Grad 1958.

Cadet William T. Reach, West Point 1959

CHAPTER FORTY-ONE

Home Ec and Homework

Well, it was the first day of ninth grade and I would finally be a true High School Student, no more Sub-Freshman. What a difference from last year, no more nerves, just excitement at seeing all my buddies again. Also, I was really looking forward to being a Twirlette on the field at half time during the football games. Oh, there would be those fun parades around the Square too.

This time I grabbed my baton in addition to the books and would be sure to use the locker as much as possible. Shay's older sister Betty agreed to take us that first day. We both felt as though we knew all the ropes of Decatur High, so hopefully we would have a no-stress day.

Yeah, my classes were pretty great that year, although some were harder than others. With my good schedule, I was pleased with the classes and various new teachers. Seeing our friends was the most fun, those guys and girls that had become a big part of our life.

I said *Hey* to Martina, Jackie, Warren, Gail, Shay, Barbara, Billy Gae, Allen, Johnny, Freddy, and cute Charles Evans. There were also new friends from the Twirlette squad. With all the practicing over the summer, the trek between buildings seemed like a snap. My favorite part of the day was the gathering in front of the middle building with friends and sit on the rock wall to talk over things, maybe even flirt a bit here and there.

My second class of the day was in the South Building in Home Ec class with Mrs. Folger. This was going to be fun I thought, because I already knew a bit about sewing and cooking. Mother had also taught me how to embroider on pillowcases and handkerchiefs with delicate flowers of all colors. It was fun, who knew I would like this type of handwork. Mama had even smiled at my progress which made my embroidering even better.

Walking into the Home Ec room that first day was a surreal experience, no desks. There was a big bright kitchen with gleaming white cabinets. Also, four or five large white tables with red stools were in the center of the room. It looked like our kitchen at home but blown way out to a huge proportion. Beyond that was a row of sewing machines. Oh no, they were all those devil treadle machines that took too much foot power.

I spotted my friend Gail Carrington; she smiled and waved. Gail was very pretty, taller than me and had light brown hair with soft curls. I was proud to have her as my friend.

"Now girls there will not be a lot of talking and visiting in this class," Mrs. Folger admonished to us giggling girls. Then she smiled and added, "But we are going to learn a lot of fun things like cooking and sewing that you will really enjoy." I liked her.

Gail and I grabbed two stools at one of the big tables. There were maybe twenty girls in the class, guess the boys thought it was too sissy to take Home Ec, not cool enough. They missed seeing the cute girls in this class.

"We will jump right into our first project which will be to bake a dozen biscuits for each of you. All the recipes will be handed out, then you can each come up to get your ingredients and return to your table."

There were mixing bowls, measuring cups, big wooden spoons, cookie sheet pans, even aprons for each of us. Four girls to each of the five tables. Gail and I had made sure we were at the same table. Both of us had helped our mothers make biscuits but never had made them by ourselves. It was different, it was harder.

Flour seemed to be everywhere. We shared the rolling pin, and it was soon *gunky* with a flour and milk paste. I did not like messes and would clean it off each time I used it, putting me behind. All of us managed to get our biscuits on the pans and into the ovens. From that point there were squeals like, "Oh no mine are burning, oh, I set the temperature too high" and "Oh no, mine are not rising, just spreading out, oops, I forgot the baking soda." It was funny to hear all of this.

Mine were not burnt and they did rise, but they were not soft and fluffy like Mama's. Gail's were a little better and tastier than mine. It was fun and funny to see all the different shades and shapes of biscuits. We made mistakes but learned from them.

At lunch that day I managed to locate Shay, Martina, Billy Gae and Jean. Then Gail, Ann Bentley and Nina Gae joined us. We had chats and laughs over lunch, mainly laughing over our own mistakes made that morning in classes. The afternoon was Latin, Algebra and Gym class. We played basketball, all hating our one-piece blue shorts outfits. Surprisingly, I played much better at basketball than last year. It must have been all the baton practices over the summer. After the end of the class day there was a Twirlette practice at school. Busy, Busy.

In our Home Ec class, there were more cooking hits and cooking misses of cookies, cakes, and pies before we began our sewing classes. Since there were not enough machines, we staggered the use of them. We made aprons with a button on bib top and pockets on the bottom. I really liked cutting the cloth with the patterns and pinning those pieces together. Some were better than others, some were never completed, and some girls had bloody fingers from sticking themselves with the pins and needles.

I really had worked hard to sew my project nicely so Mother could see I was trying to learn. It turned out kind of cute. I even embroidered my name on the top part, surprisingly neat. And we all had our share of leg cramps from those dreadful Treadle Sewing Machines.

Well into the school year, Mrs. Quinn came to our Home Ec classroom to announce there would be a Sewing Contest. At the conclusion, we would be in a fashion show where we would each wear our own completed outfits.

Smiles and grins everywhere. We were each improving so making an outfit would be fun.

"Now girls, this contest is meant to challenge you to try some difficult styles with good fabric so your finished outfits should look polished."

Mrs. Quinn then added, "You will pick out the fabric and the patterns to your liking. But keep in mind that points will be added for complicated stitches and features. Perhaps difficult pleats in the skirts, buttoned cuffs on blouses, gussets or even the French stitch on collars would all add points."

Murmurs "What is a gusset or a French collar anyway?" Could be heard. Mrs. Quinn added that Mrs. Folger would help us and she herself would also be around at times to answer any of our questions.

She then asked, "How does that sound?" as she looked all around to see our responses. Silence, then, "Oh, Fun," I blurted out too loudly, then was embarrassed.

Mrs. Quinn smiled and said she appreciated my enthusiasm and looked forward to seeing my finished outfit. *Oh Boy, now what had I done?* She would be expecting me to do well.

Gail was giggling behind her hands, so I said, "Yes, Ma'am, I will try to do a great job on my outfit." We both smiled.

That project turned out to be a lot of homework because Mother and I went to Rich's to look at patterns and fabric. It was great fun, but confusing. After much looking, feeling the fabric to test the quality as Mama had shown me over the years, we finally made a decision. My skirt would be a straight burnt-orange wool with a fancy double pleat in the back. The long-sleeved cuffed blouse would have a French collar in a cotton satin paisley print in soft colors.

It was hard, difficult, and I became discouraged. The intricate pattern had about a million pieces to cut out and then pin to the fabric before I could even begin sewing. What had I gotten myself into with this doggone complicated outfit? But I forged ahead and took Mama's advice to do a little at a time to not be overwhelmed. I did just that, it worked. Mama was always right.

That Freshman year seemed to fly by with all the activities and fun. Dating was now part of my world, let me say, my super-duper world. Car dates were a big deal, and it seemed my social life had blossomed. Those cute boys were asking me out on dates, walking me home, sometimes carrying my books between classes. That must have been what all the hullabaloo about high school was, guys and girls dating and just having fun together.

Then the time came for our Home Ec Fashion show. All of us had finally completed our outfits and looked pretty sharp with our hair done, wearing stockings and pretty shoes along with nervous smiles. There was a wide variety of outfits, some made dresses long or short, fancy or conservative, many had made skirts and blouses as Gail, and I had done.

It was a bit nerve wracking to parade in front of the panel of judges. Gee, I didn't know it was going to be such a big deal After a few failed attempts at trying a fashionable walk, I just slowly walked by with a smile, after all we were not models. Then they studied closely our sewing techniques, zippers installed, buttonholes made well, seams and hems straight and all that kind of detailed perfection.

We were glad it was over and glad we had a rather good time showing them our sewing triumphs. Well, you will never believe it, I won the contest. Me, using my hands well and not like writing on blackboards in Cursive when my letters slanted down to the floor. I beamed as I was told *Well Done* and received an engraved Silver Thimble with its own case. Mama would be proud.

At last, I found something I could do well, sewing. But embroidery and knitting were fun also.

CHAPTER FORTY-TWO

Dating, Dancing, and Dreaming

"Shay, do you realize what a terrific year this is?" I asked. "Look at all the friends we have made and boys we have met to be able to date and go to dances with them. I mean it is pretty great."

We had just played a game of Badminton in her back yard. Shay had gotten us some lemonade and as we sat, just started talking about our Freshman year at Decatur High. Shay had remained my best friend and the one I confided in about the ups and downs and sometimes frowns of High School and being teenagers. I am not sure I could have gotten through those years without her.

Shay nodded and said, "Yeah, we are really doing super fun things this year. And you have already gone on car dates, you lucky girl. My birthday is soon, and I will be able to car date too."

I laughed out loud and shook my head. "Let me tell you, it did not happen easily, in fact I thought no one would ever ask me out on a real car date, ever. I made the mistake of telling Mama how discouraged I was."

"Uh Oh, and just how well did that remark go?" Shay asked with a giggle.

"Oh, she immediately had an idea of course. She said she would make me a sign to hang on my back to say, 'Judy Can Car Date Now.' Can you believe that?"

As things turned out, it was not necessary to advertise myself. The very next week I was asked out on a double date with Charles Evans, who had a friend with his own car. We went to a movie, then to a drive-in for some French Fries and Cokes. It was all wonderful fun and the four of us had a super time. I was happy and felt a little bit independent on that first car date Saturday night.

My social life was in full swing, and I was doing well with my studies. I made the honor roll and was selected to the Student Council. My friend Gail Carrington was voted VP of our Freshman class, Freddy Wheeler was President, Molly Sargent Secretary, and Johnny McCamman treasurer.

One of my favorite and fun things that happened was that in the school newspaper, the *Scribbler*, I had been voted the *Wittiest*. Well, that made me happy. Last year I was the *Friendliest*, probably because I flashed a smile and a Hi to everyone I passed here and there. Now that people knew me better, they realized I had a good sense of humor, it meant they really knew me, not just the smile and a wave.

"Julian Price just asked me on a date," I hesitantly said to my mother. "He was one of Tommy's friends, Mama," I excitedly blurted out too quickly.

"Oh Judy, I don't know, isn't he much older than you?" she quickly responded.

I forged ahead, "You remember him, Tommy brought him over to the house several times." Still a blank face. "You know, he was the polite guy with the red hair." Bingo.

"Oh goodness, of course, that nice looking young man with the beautiful red hair who looked as though he was Irish," and she nodded her head and beamed. Success.

The best part of this whole date was that Julian was taking me to the East Lake Country Club for dinner. How cool was that?

Julian arrived in a big, sleek car looking quite handsome in his suit and tie topped off with a tie clip and cuff links. I smiled as I noticed Daddy checking out his shoes, his highly polished dress shoes. Guess Julian passed from head to toe. He also presented me with a wrist corsage. It topped off my lavender dress with the green duster jacket and high heels. We both looked nice.

After we pulled up to the entrance of the East Lake Country Club, the Valet opened my door. He told Julian he would park his car. Looking over at the golf course and the fence along the road, a vivid memory popped into my head. There I had been, leaning on the handlebars of my bike thinking, "I will be going to that impressive club one day on the arm of a nice guy." Here I was.

We had a delicious dinner with an attentive waiter. The table was beautifully set with white linens, sterling silverware, fine China, crystal, and flowers in the center with a candle, perfect. I was glad to have learned charm and manners, so I felt comfortable. This was a lovely place that was filled with fine furnishings and mahogany walls. Julian was sweet, polite, and a lot of fun. He later asked me out to the movies and to a dance, he was just a super guy.

When Twerp Week came around all us girls had a chance to ask the boys out for a change. I took the opportunity to ask Warren to a movie and Johnny Mac to the Sadie Hawkins Day Dance. It was a whirlwind week of fun. I made a corsage for Johnny Mac after the Russian Sputnik, the first small satellite to circle the Earth. We could see it pass over on clear nights.

I cut a Styrofoam ball in half, stuck big blue bubblegum balls to it with toothpicks, finished off with a cute blue bow. The dance was great fun, especially since people kept coming up to Johnny to pull off a gum ball. It was all very cool. Johnny was a good dancer and always fun to be with, so Twerp Week was a fine week indeed.

The year seemed to fly too quickly to do all the things that needed to be done. There were Slumber Parties given by Jan Hambright, Jeanne Bellville, Pat Grogan, and others. There were usually giggles, goodies, and guys stopping by for the perfect formula of a successful party, and lots of Christmas parties and a surprise birthday party for Jackie Hamilton. Oh, he was a good slow dancer and I really enjoyed being around him. He and Warren Neal were buddies; what a couple of cuties.

Warren had quickly passed by the cute stage and gone directly to handsome. One whiff of English Leather cologne would send me reeling. Oh Geeze-o-Pete, what was wrong with me? Where were my brothers when I needed guidance? Looked as though I was on my own and not a good source for sane judgement. I must keep that ever inviting but dangerous Pandora's Box tightly shut, too many temptations.

Shay and I had another girl talk, but we were in the same boat on the same sea of dating adventures. Both of us knew we had to keep our moral standards, which was important. Could that mind set be the reason I did not have boyfriends that lasted too long? But I was not going to drop my self-respect or values.

Charles Evans soon became my boyfriend; he was a good-looking guy who made my heartbeat faster. When I saw him from a distance and our eyes met, I would break out a big smile. He made me swoon. We were named New Steadies in the Scribbler. It was wonderful. We went to movies, the Varsity, the Rec Center, even a hayride to Stone Mountain.

Of course, it was too good to be true to last for very long. He found a girl he liked, then I found other boys who were also cute and nice after we broke up. Did I have a fickle heart? Did I flirt too much? Maybe, but I did shed many tears over that breakup, my heart hurt for a while.

There was much to learn about this dating game. I will have to practice more, surely that would help.

Judy's Movies and Dates in 1958 and 1959:

Bell book and Candle • *Restless Years*, Dick Eichoff • *Battle Hymn*, Charles Evans • The Ten *Commandments* • *The Geisha Girl* at the Roxy Theater, a triple date with Warren, me, Johnny Mac, Nina Gae, Freddy, Martina then to the Varsity • *Auntie Mame*, Shay, Betty, Nikki, me • *Sing Boy Sing Tell Tale Heart Vertigo*

Dances

Sock Hop with David Popwell • The Sophomore Dance with Ikey Cobb The ROTC Ball with Richard Plant • GMAC Dance with Butch Luther Sadie Hawkins Dance with Johnny McCamman • a Senior Dance with Julian Price and more!

My circle of friends continued to grow, and I continued to enjoy my seventh-grade College Heights friends. Billy Gae Selman and I had become good friends and buddies. She lived close by our house on McDonough at the end of Lenore, that downhill road we skated and biked down. In fact, if we had ever missed stopping our downhill roll before the busy McDonough Street, we would have landed right in her front lawn.

Billy Gae had blond hair, a big smile and laughed at my jokes. What more could you ask from a friend? Oh, she like to twirl the baton just as our friend Jeanne Bellville did. We went to Slumber Parties with them and Janet Blalock from that class too. Good friends, good fun and twirling.

We had one very special day at Decatur High called Blue-Jeans Day where even the girls got to wear them. After only skirts and dresses, believe me, wearing blue jeans was great. Billy Gae, Janet, Jeanne, and I decided to go to the new Rec Center that day. This was a step up from the small Canteen we had before, because there were more pool tables, plus trampolines, mats for tumbling, even a basketball court. The best part was the snack bar and music for dancing on the large dance floor, which we did quite frequently. That Blue Jean Day we could play and dance without our skirts flying this, that, and the up-too-high way.

After a little while, more kids joined us, making it almost a party that unusual day. Neal Pharr, Larry Abbey, Shay, Billy Gae, Gail, JohnnyMac, Allen, Warren, Jackie, Freddy, Phoebe, Martha Erdman, Patsy Guinn, Martina, Johnny and others showed up at the Rec Center that day. We decided to have a dance contest, and would you believe Johnny Mac and I won that contest. While we were dancing, in walked Sandy Ballengee, Barbara Archer, Ann Bentley, Allen Calloway, Nina Gae Miller, and of course Charles Evans. I think we almost exploded the Rec Center with Decatur High Freshmen that day.

It was all too wonderful. It was making my Memories. Once again, I was just where I should be and with whom I should be, my Dear Decatur Friends. Thank you everyone.

Surely these days of Dancing, Dating and Dreams coming true would be forever memorable.

Freshman Class Student Council

Virginia Harris, David Popwell, Johnny Lyons, Gail Carrington Warren Neal, Barbara Archer, Martha Erdman, Judy Tatum

CHAPTER FORTY-THREE

No, No, No to Moving

During those whirlwind days and exciting dating games, my family had more changes. Kenny had been dating Gail Brown for a while now, which was fine with me, she was pretty and fun. It was great to have her to talk to like a sister and things were getting serious between them. Kenny had moved back home and taken a good new job.

There seemed to be a revolving door for me to go through to get that big corner room. I had been in it for the few months since Tommy left for West Point and Kenny was living at his Oglethorpe apartment. Instead of the pass-through bedroom off the kitchen and hallway, this bedroom was in its own corner of the house. It had big windows that allowed me to see more, even a little bit of McKoy Park. That bedroom was a sunny, cozy nest with only one door instead of three. It was fun to watch the walkers, bikers, drivers and doggies that passed by that side of our house.

Then in January of 1959, Kenny and Gail decided to get married, and they did. It was very exciting and neat o for me to have a pretty new sister-in-law nearer my age, especially since Gail and Kenny were going to live with us until they found a house. I didn't mind going back to the 3-door bedroom, after all I had my own entrance to the porch and back yard. It was worth it.

They did find a house in a month or two off Glenwood close to Tony Valley where Patsy and Tommy's first house was located. It was a brick home that sparkled inside with a huge fenced in back yard. Smoky could run around and play and not run away. Smokey was our dog Eno's brother. Eno had grown into a large goofy great dog. Kenny and Gail were headed to a happy life together in their new home.

Of course, I was back in the big room, but would it last? I decided to take that bedroom situation day by day and enjoy where I was and when I was. The sad thing was that it seemed it would now be just Daddy, Mama, and me. However, there was a great deal going on at school now with busy classes, too much homework, and twirling here and there as we were needed. There was also the all-important socializing that made my days long and packed full of activities.

Then one April Saturday, Daddy asked me to have a talk in the Living Room. *What did I do?* Daddy never had a talk with just me, especially in the Living Room, for Goodness Sakes. This was going to be grim. My heart started racing as I sat down on the couch and Daddy sat on the couch too, not in his chair. *Not a good sign.*

He saw the panic in my face and flashed me one of his warm smiles and patted my hand. I did breathe a little easier…until he started talking.

"Judy, I know you have been hearing whispers and talking going on around here lately," he stated.

"Oh, no, Daddy I never try to hear anything I should not know." Even as those words came out of my mouth, they should have gone right into the trash can. Everyone knew we all listened here and there to learn anything we should not hear. I felt my face turn red.

But he laughed, I loved his laugh. "Of course, you don't, but I wanted to clear up anything you have heard about my job."

Oh that, that thing I did not want to hear about and just blocked it from my brain. However, my brain was filled with a runaway imagination, so I had been worried. I did not speak.

"Let me tell you just what has happened. You are fifteen now and can understand," he said.

My head was thinking, *Nope I am not able to understand anything, and I mess up all the time.*

"Yes, Sir," I managed to whisper.

A new administration came into the Capitol Building that meant there would be some sweeping changes," he softly uttered.

My eight-year-old brain thought, can't they find new sweepers? But my fifteen-year-old mouth said, "Oh, Daddy, don't tell me you are losing your Revenue Agent job?"

"Yes, that is exactly what has already happened. We have some big decisions to make," he paused a little too long before continuing. This would only get worse.

"Your Mother and I have decided it is time for me to retire from government work."

Retire, doesn't that mean to not work anymore and what would he do now? I thought.

"What that means is, we want to move back to Florida where we started out our marriage. Also, Roy, Patsy and Kenny were born in Florida," he said.

Yep, once again Tommy and I, the two youngest who were born in Waycross, Georgia were not in the majority, I think to myself, then say, "But, Daddy, I want to graduate from Decatur High. I have many friends and making good grades and all..." I trailed off seeing his face, his sad face.

After a few seconds he said, "Look, you need to think about all this, and your mother and I will answer any questions you will have. Let's not talk anymore right now."

The horror of my realizing what was going to happen bought bright tears to my eyes, he saw that. Quietly I sat there with my hands clenched in my lap trying not to cry, "Okay."

I continued to sit after he left. My overactive imagination was started to do its work, I was about to go nuts. This could not be happening. They cannot break up my friends and my whole life. No, no, no to moving.

Mama finally came in to see if I was all right. My sorrowful face and watery eyes told her, exactly. No words were needed, so she sat by me. "Judy, we know this is a big blow for you, but these are life changing circumstances that we have to deal with, and soon."

She was using big words in a complicated sentence to try and throw me off, but I was determined to sulk and be upset. There were too many thoughts about consequences and outcomes, oh no, now I was thinking in big words. *Get hold of yourself and say something.*

"Mama, can't I just stay with Kenny and Gail? They would not mind that would they?" Yes, I began to grasp at straws, "I can help around the house and do my own laundry and ironing and maybe even help cook." The straws I was trying to grasp had turned into limp noodles.

"Now Honey, think that through, they cannot take you to and from school each day. It is a long drive to your high school from their house." There she was, being practical and smart again.

Pushing ahead, "Yea, but I get my driver's license this year you know," her face said it all.

"You don't have a car and they only have one, right?" Man, she already knew everything.

Trying a new tactic, my teen brain had another good idea. "Well, Shay, I mean Shay's family, they would love to have me stay with them." Still grasping, still slipping away.

She just shook her head. Nothing was working. My boat was paddling upstream with only a wooden spoon to row the boat. What can I do? Nothing, I could not do another thing to make this moving crisis go better for me. I was doomed.

I began telling my friends what was going to happen that summer. Shay was the first one I told this dreadful news; that was when my tears began to flow, as did hers. It was hard to take, hard to hear, harder to grasp the true fallout from this move to Florida in a few months.

The school year would be ending soon so there were plenty of busy times. I had slowly begun to tell more friends that I would not be here for our sophomore year. There were tears, warm hugs, and a few smiles thinking about visiting me in Florida.

Mother and Daddy and I took off in our big Buick to begin a house hunt, starting on the west coast of Florida around the Tampa-St. Petersburg area. It was beautiful there and I was enjoying the traveling part, but each house we looked at made me sad. I could not picture living in any home that was not in Decatur, Georgia.

Mother and Daddy had met below Melbourne, Florida while she was a teacher in a one-room schoolhouse and Daddy was doing work with the Border Patrol. They had married near there and continued to move around with his job, from Miami, Melbourne, New Smyrna and even Daytona Beach. Roy, Patsy, and Kenny were born in Florida, each in a different city. I was realizing that they still had a tug at their hearts for the East Coast. We had taken two-week vacations in both Daytona and New Smyrna.

Our next trip covered a large area and too many homes in too many towns, but finally there was one in Ormond Beach, north of Daytona that was fairly new and kinda' cute. It was two blocks from the Halifax River and just across the bridge to that beautiful Atlantic Ocean and white sand. I was still pouting a bit, yet liked that house, but it was too small with a small yard. It was perfect for a retired couple, not perfect for the teenage me.

That was the one they chose. The writing on my *wall of life* was being written in big black messy letters: *Life is over as you know it, face that fact.*

CHAPTER FORTY- FOUR

'Til We Meet Again

As the school year was coming to an end, the 1959 Yearbooks arrived. It was very cool to take it everywhere with me to have my friends sign with messages. Many of them said they would come down to see me on their Easter Breaks. Daytona Beach was the choice location for teenage trips, so there was one glimmer of hope to see my friends sometimes. It would never be the same though.

My *Summer of the Great Sulk and Snit* was going strong. Now I could pout masterfully but having no brothers to notice my pout wasn't the same. I was just left with an overwhelming emptiness.

It was not *good-bye* to all my friends, but a *see you later*. Several buddies told me they would visit me in Florida especially if we were going to live near an ocean. Even thinking about those visits, the reality of this big change was really setting into my brain, and my heart.

When my nose began to get back into joint, I tried to be more positive…where was Shay to talk over this Monumental Heartbreak? Well, she soon did come down for a whole week. We talked, laughed, went to movies, played putt-putt golf and went to the ocean. My smile returned, my joy resurfaced, and happiness crept into my broken heart. Yes, very dramatic.

Sure enough, Jackie Hamilton and Warren Neal also came to Daytona Beach. We enjoyed the beach and ocean and just hung out like friends. They will always stay in my heart, it was wonderful. Also, Gail Carrington's family vacationed nearby so she and I were able to have nice beach visits. I knew it would never be the same but thinking of seeing some of my friends sometimes eased my hurt.

Living near a beautiful beach with fun places to see and things to do turned out to be quite nice. There was also the Beach Boardwalk with rides, games and concerts and we could drive cars on the beach. Well, my life was not ruined after all. I just needed to shift my brain with new positive things.

If I ever needed memories, I could open my big red scrapbook of *Judy's Jazzy Stuff*. There were pressed flowers, dance cards, party invitations, menus, ticket stubs and pictures. I also had my well-kept diaries with all kinds of good stuff to read and memories saved.

I was going to survive. Maybe happiness will find me after all, to make my life complete.

Shay and Judy at Ormond Beach

A Follow up Story

My life in Ormond Beach and at Seabreeze High school turned out much better than I had imagined. I just needed to turn the page. There I found new friends to add to my Decatur friends, never replace them. It did not happen immediately, but it did happen.

The High School was in Daytona Beach just two blocks away from the ocean, three blocks from the Boardwalk. Temptations were everywhere, not the rather tame and conservative attitudes at Decatur High in the 1950s.

In time I had friends, good friends, my circles were a little smaller. I tried to be friendly, but the big smiles and cuteness did not work there. I needed to shift my ways of approaching everyone without losing my own way of life. There was no Tommy to ask for help, Kenny's humor was not around. I realized it was time to wake up and be my own person, looking toward the future instead of trying to regain my past.

That gradually worked due to my good friend Rita McCann and Paula Tucker and Ginger Blanford taking me under their wings. They helped ease me into the Seabreeze High School style, and it worked. I gradually did have dates, went to a few dances, was asked to join the Sub Deb Club, worked in the office, and even found a few boyfriends. They did not last long though. I definitely was a southern girl with conservative ways, but that was not going to change. I would learn to adapt without changing my values.

The biggest blow was that I could not be a Majorette as they were required to play a musical instrument. The band was the *famous* Marching 100, for the Seabreeze Sandcrabs with only eight Majorettes. Wow! They were impressive. I did hang out and twirl with some of them for fun.

Mother and Daddy could not have been more understanding about my emotions. They let me have the big sunny bedroom and even gave me their mahogany four-poster bed, chest, and desk. I was in a little bit of heaven right there.

Then three-miracles happened that made me reset my emotions to have a full grasp of reality on my new life. First was that my Granny Ashley moved to Ormond Beach to live in the Big white Ormond Hotel. It was quite grand enough for *Miss Lily*. Her sister Helen also had a room on the same floor. I adored them both, so visits were often to see them on the veranda. Those sisters could watch the river while rocking and enjoying themselves. I happily joined them.

Second, was that my brother Tommy came for a long visit during a West Point break. I hugged him long and tightly so the memory would last of his visit. We laughed and had fun times together because he was happy and relaxed. My parents smiled as Tommy brought his joy and warm humor into our lives. That visit started to fill the empty hole in my heart.

The third wonderful miracle was that my brother Kenny and his wife Gail also came down for a visit bringing their first baby. Janet Lynn Reach was a happy, beautiful, precious addition to the Reach Family. Our family being together here in our Florida home brought not just happiness to Mother and Daddy, but a much-needed peace to me.

Since Daddy had retired, his pace of life was much easier. He and I would walk the two blocks to the Halifax River to enjoy the boats, the breeze, and the beauty. It seemed Daddy and I had reached a new dynamic in our life, for we finally had a father-daughter relationship. It was a joy to talk and laugh with him. His blue eyes seemed to sparkle as he looked at the river and boats.

Even going to the beach was special with my parents. Mother smiled more, hugged more, and just like Daddy, was more relaxed. While Daddy and I floated on the waves, Mother kept a diligent watch over us to be sure the tide did not take us too far away. We would hear, "Roy, Judy, come back to shore." Her voice carried well over the sounds of the waves.

Daddy was at peace, that was it. My funny, kind, sweet, bright daddy had found that place of joy. The love my parents had for each other shone through as they walked. They would be arm in arm, heads together, laughing and sharing their little jokes. I was glad to have been able to share those easy, relaxed times with Mother and Daddy. They looked younger and happier.

Our smaller family's life was good. My life was getting better. I could begin to move forward.

Judy, Gail, Proud granddaddy with Janet, Mama,
Granny Ashley, Kenny and Tommy in back

287

Race of Time

It takes a lot to slow us down
To calm our always hurried pace.

It takes a lot to turn us around
And look behind in this mad race.

Sometimes it may be a gentle pull
That slows our hurry to a halt.

Sometimes it may be a little lull
To let us see this one small fault.

But someday the moment will come
when time will tell us true,

To stop and meditate upon
Our past and present too.

Judy Reach
1966

Roy Reach, Sr. and Libby Ashley Family Lineage

Roy Wheeler Reach, Sr (1904-1969) and Elizabeth (Libby) Ashley

- They had Roy Jr, Patsy, Kenny, Tommy, and Judy

1) Roy Reach, Jr. (1930-1997) wed Margie Barrow

- They had Steve, Bob, David, Russell, Tom, Ronald
- Steve Reach wed MaryAnn
- Bob Reach wed Julie, had Kelley, Jesse, Jacob
- David married Jane, had Dylan, then David wed Lauren had Ryan
- Russell Reach (1957-2007) wed Beth,
- They had Emily, Phillip, Rebekah, Daniel, Sarah, and Abbey
- Dr. Tom Reach wed Darlene had Julie, Andy, Tim, Jennifer
- Then Tom married Marguerite, had El
- Ronald married Sloan, had Windsor

2) Patsy Reach wed Tommy Cullens, had Tom, Cathy, and Patti.

- Cathy Cullens wed Dave Bame (1945-2015), had Katie and Cary Anne
- Katie Bame wed Angelo Bravo, had son Brooks
- Cary Anne Bame married Brett Falconer
- Patti Cullens wed Donald Burch, had Trey and Patricia

3) Kenny Reach wed Gail Brown (1942-2003) had Janet, Ken Jr, Cindy

- Janet Reach wed Dell Keith, had Katie and Kerrie
- Katie Keith wed Chris Cowart, had Aubrey, Ashton, Lexi
- Kerrie Keith wed Marshal Rogne, had Emmaline, Kinsey, Tayton
- Ken, Jr wed Susan, had Libby, Evan, Jack, Cate
- Libby Reach wed Erik Matheison, had Olivia
- Evan Reach wed Lena had Emmett

- Jack Reach wed Kristen, had Lorelei

- Cate Reach wed Mike Miller, had Henry

- Cindy Reach wed Rodger Rehorn, had Austin, Ansley, Tyler

- Austin Rehorn wed Erica

- Ansley Rehorn wed Brando Ellison, had Everleigh, Boston

- Tyler Rehorn, girlfriend Sydney Lee

4) Lt. Tommy Reach (1940-1965) wed Rosemary Kistler, had William T. Jr. (Bill)

- Bill Reach wed and had Amelia

5) Judy Reach wed Bob LaRocca, had Beth, Tony, Len

- Beth LaRocca wed Joseph Stearman had Michael, Christopher

- Tony LaRocca, Jr, married Tracy Wright, had Nicholas, Katie

- Len Reach Jacobs wed Keith Cumbie had Jacob, Amy

About the Author

Judy Reach LaRocca presently lives in Saint Johns, Florida, near Jacksonville with her husband Bob who, she thanks for his forever patience, organization, and encouragement. Most of all for sharing his enduring love for almost 55 years. She now has the time to enjoy her life while sharing her stories with others, especially her three grown children and six grandchildren. Family is everything in life.

Decatur Stories: The 1950s with Judy, is filled with fun and charming tales of her pre-teen and teen years with her Reach family of seven in North Georgia. Each chapter is a short story with dialogue both humorous and touching, all based on her actual life. Maybe just a pinch of salt is added for flavor. A touch of humor, a bit of reality, and a lot of family love.

Her writings include Books, Life Stories with Humor, Short Stories, Poems and Prose, and now Fairy Tales. Her series of books *Reaching for Life* began with her first published work *Judy's Story of Waycross*. This tells about her early childhood in a South Georgia town, a booming railroad hub during its prime in the 1940s. Her last published book *The Adventures of Benji, Pansy and Herzhog,* has given joy and fun for children to grandparents. Filled with mystical and magical creatures such as Fizzle BoomDiggle, Harry HobGob, and Sherriff Bertram BumbleHauser, each with their own story. www.JudysStory.com

Remember: "A touch of humor along the path of life makes the journey easier."